INTRODUCTION TO THE
SACRAMENTS

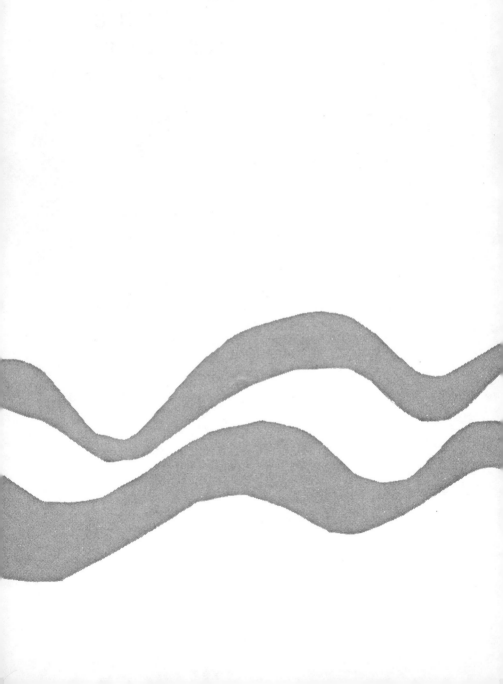

INTRODUCTION TO THE SACRAMENTS

JOHN P. SCHANZ

Pueblo Publishing Company
New York

Citations from Odo Casel, *The Mystery of Christian Worship* (Westminster, Md.: Newman Press, 1962), courtesy of Paulist Press.

Scriptural pericopes are quoted from the New American Bible.

Design: Br. Aelred-Seton Shanley

ISBN: 0-916134-57-1

To my devoted and generous Cousin
MARIA WESCHLER
whose long teaching career has continued
a family tradition
that I too have been privileged
to follow

Contents

Introduction

One's faith life inevitably comes to focus in community. In this framework, the solitary Christian experiences the sustaining, inspiring, and transforming power that galvanizes individual faith into communal commitment.

John Donne's axiomatic "No man is an island" has a particular relevance to Christian worship. It is in public, communal worship that we Christians discover who we are—the people of God—and grow into an awareness of what we are to become—a family bonded to one another in Christ. Public worship focuses our vision on the glorified Lord, realizes his sacramental presence in our midst, and energizes us to convert our petty individualism into a true *koinonia*, a fellowship in Christ.

To this end the present study was undertaken. It emerged from the initial enthusiasm of Vatican II, whose *Constitution on the Sacred Liturgy* (1963) charted a liturgical renascence in the Catholic Church still not entirely fulfilled. The present work is an outgrowth of the author's earlier *Sacraments of Life and Worship* (Bruce, 1966), one of a series of postconciliar texts oriented to the mature Catholic and collegiate scene.

In the intervening years, the postconciliar Consilium or commission on liturgical revision has published new manuals of worship for all the sacraments. Litur-

gical directives have sought to implement a radical
faith renewal of the Church's prayer life, but texts and
rubrics alone will not suffice. A holistic attitude must
be formed to translate static formulas into living
prayer.

Furthermore, theology has not been stagnant since the
Council. A wholly new impetus launched theological reflection into a major revival based upon a significant
thrust in human consciousness, what Bernard Lonergan called a shift from classicism to *historical consciousness*.[1] Such a change of context has profoundly affected
the way of doing theology today. No longer are we
satisfied with an essentialist, static, immutable world
view. Ours is a more flexible, existentialist, emergent,
anthropologically based theology that listens with one
ear to the divine utterance of historical revelation and
keeps the other open to the problematic of contemporary existence, with all its queries, challenges, and
enigmas. In short, today's Christian is more open to a
type of correlation theology that moves from the contemporary human situation—as interpreted by current
philosophical, anthropological, psychological, and
social-scientific reflection—to the revelatory level to
probe the mystery of what God is saying to us today in
our existential situation.

Accordingly, this exposition of sacramental theology
seeks to organize sacramental thinking along currently
viable procedural lines. Beginning with an analysis of
religion and ritual worship as a constant in human life
designed to interpret and celebrate the core meaning
of existence (Chapter 1), we proceed to discuss the central pattern of symbolic or "sacramental" thinking, dis-
cernible in the human tendency to express one's most
fundamental human feelings in a tangible way as a
bond of communication with others. Man's instinctive
sensitivities for human intercommunion are authenti-

cated by the biblical statement of a God who communicates himself to us in order to reorient estranged humankind to a loving Father by the gift of his own Son (Chapter 2), who gathers up sinful, fragmented humanity into a new family emerging out of Jesus' paschal self-donation. Israel's "stories of God," told and retold in rite and Scripture, achieve a new actuality in water baptism and sacrifice-meal, as saving history comes to a climax in a sacramentally grounded church, in the light of which we essay to evolve a tentative or working definition of *sacrament* (Chapter 3). The law of history is dialogue, as God and man meet in a symbolic encounter that transcends body limitation and signals a whole world open to divine love proclaiming itself in the life-giving word of sacramental celebration (Chapter 4). Chapter 5 shows the sacraments as realization or "actualization" of Christ's saving acts, aimed at renewing humanity through a nuclear center that lives by word and sacrament. Chapter 6 compares various sacramental models and introduces the new model of "celebration."

Ours then is an exciting challenge, a venture into "sonar" theology, sounding out the Spirit's message to the Church of the 1980s and the Church of the centuries encoded in word and worship, ever ancient, ever new. Discerning the Spirit, therefore, requires due concern for the historical framework within which his promptings occur. The Church's rich theological heritage has not been ignored in this study, as we move from the revealed data through the patristic, Augustinian, medieval, and Thomistic traditions to a contemporary understanding of sacraments. In this way, the sense of a developing theological corpus is better preserved, the process of investigation better understood.

It is hoped that the present volume serves an introductory function: to examine the anthropological, biblical, traditional, and historico-theological base upon which an integral sacramental theology can be constructed.

NOTE

1. Bernard J.F. Lonergan, S.J. *Method in Theology* (New York: Herder and Herder, 1972), p. 301f.

The Framework of Sacraments: Religion and Worship

It is impossible to speak meaningfully of Christian sacraments without first locating them in their proper context. It should be obvious to anyone versed in Christianity that sacraments are some kind of *religious* acts—that is, they are actions by which one tries to communicate with God, to show one's relationship to him, to pay him homage, and to receive some kind of benefit from him in return. Thus to center sacraments in their most general field of human experience, we must first attempt to understand more exactly what *religion* means and what it implies to say that *worship* is a central expression of *religion*.

ETYMOLOGICAL DEFINITION OF RELIGION

While it is recognized that the word "religion" is a Latin derivative, no general consensus exists as to its precise roots. Several proposals have been suggested. Cicero mentions *relegere*, "constantly to turn to"; *retractare*, "to take up again, renew"; and *religari*, "binding oneself back to something, that is, to one's primary purpose"; and *reeligere*, "to go back to one's primary purpose after having drifted away from it."

Cicero, principally in his *De Natura Deorum (On the Nature of the Gods)*, tried to put some order into the diverse notions that the Romans had about their gods and the honor to be paid to them. At first he seemed to use the word "religion" to mean "the outward observance of a particular practice," not merely toward the gods, but also toward other persons. Under his tutelage the word principally "accumulated the highly charged notional connotation and subjective reference that we associate not primarily with the ritual but with the transcendent reality in whose name the ritual is observed."[1]

The word "religion" is thus the work of the Greco-Roman mind that seems to have wanted to distinguish the cultic aspect of the Roman worship of the gods from the social activities of the state. This was a gigantic step in a way for early peoples; for example, the Egyptians made no distinction between their social life and their worship life. "[B]oth institutionally and in personal feeling 'religion' was not separated off as a particular."[2] There is no word for religion, for example, in the Old Testament.

The etymology of the word "religion" is valid only in Latin, but the rich vein of concepts that Cicero unearthed is still being mined by anthropologists, social scientists, theologians, and historians down to the present day. As Smith says, "Cicero's work contributed . . . to the development of a notion of religion as a generic something in human life that is an attitude or practice of reverence and due diligence toward the gods . . . and something interior to persons."[3]

RELIGION ACCORDING TO THE SOCIAL SCIENCES
As we turn to the social and anthropological sciences for their understanding of religion,[4] it is well to observe that the competence of these sciences in the field of religion is largely limited to a descriptive and interpretative analysis of human experience. The social scientist, as such, is not concerned with judging values or truths in religious structures, but simply with analyzing the historical and cultural forms of human religious practice. His field of interest includes the forms

and functions of ritual patterns, the influence of religious belief upon human conduct and social structures, and the psychological dimensions of religious experience. Psychology, for example, is concerned with personal experience, with the religious aspects of phenomena such as emotion, visions, dreams, and ecstasies, and with their impact on the human psyche. Sociologists of religion concern themselves with the influence of religious beliefs on societal structures, with subcultures inspired by religion, and with the impact of the cultural-social context on religion. Anthropology specializes in the primitive societal experience and is more widely cultural and ethnic in interest. These disciplines enable us to study what the empirical scientist can tell us about the nature of religion and how worship fits into the context of man's religious practice.

To the social scientist, religion appears both as a quest for and a "thrust toward or response to ultimate Power Worth."[5] Gerhard Lensky defines religion functionally as a "system of beliefs about the nature of force(s) ultimately shaping man's destiny, and the practices associated therewith, shared by members of a group."[6] Common to most of the innumerable "definitions" or descriptions of religion volunteered by the social scientist is the notion of a concern and quest for ultimacy and the response that humankind feels compelled to make to the Ultimate Mystery that grounds human existence.

From the dawn of history, humankind has evinced an interest in the absolute Other, a conviction that some ultimate force underlies the mystery of life around one. Many persons scattered throughout history have at times experienced a deep sense of a transcendent, wholly other Reality that stands over against all ordinary realities and in a sense "reveals" itself to man through the cosmos, as well as through more personal influences upon certain individuals who claim a certain experience of the supernatural. This religious consciousness or awareness of the supremely Other appears to the social scientist as a genuine experience, indicative of the basic honesty of the reporters.[7]

Apprehension of Ultimate Power

The object of religion appears first as *Power*. Primitive man was aware of his contingency, his dependency upon some ultimate Power, especially when he was faced with crises in human life such as birth and death, the powers of fire and flood, and the unleashed forces of nature.

Along with this, there is evidenced in human experience a concerted drive toward unity; that is, amid the plurality and diversity of human experience, even among those who have espoused a type of polytheism, there has been an attempt to unify human experience by tying it in with one over-arching cause. In short, man has attempted to contact that power that appears as the One, the ultimate explanation of human life in all its diverse and challenging forms.

A rather novel social-scientific approach to establishing man's belief in the ultimate is developed by Peter Berger in his work *A Rumor of Angels*.[8] Analyzing human experience, he cites examples of what he labels "signals of transcendence," pointers toward a religious interpretation of the human situation. He chooses five examples: (1) man's *propensity to order*, (2) the experience of *play*, (3) the prevalence of *hope*, (4) the expectation of *damnation* for monstrous evil, and (5) man's indulgence in *humor*.[9]

The human propensity to order reality in some way, he suggests, corresponds to an order that transcends empirical reality and encourages human beings to entrust themselves to this "supernatural" reality, whose existence may be inferred by "inductive faith." The human

4

attraction to "play" enables one to "step out of time," to bracket or suspend temporarily the harsh reality of "living toward death" (Heidegger). How could this be indulged unless there is instinctively a feeling that somehow "deathless childhood," liberation, peace, and joy will one day be vindicated by an inductive act of religious faith in the beyond.

Similarly, Berger cites man's unconquerable disposition to *hope*, even in the face of tragedy, suffering, and inevitable death. Man generally does not yield to despair, but goes on hoping for some kind of ultimate victory—he refuses to say "yes" to death as the end of all things.[10] The presence of monstrous evil in the world (wars, massacres of the innocent, etc.) seems to call for a punishment transcending this life—a hell, a damnation![11]

Finally, citing the "archetypes" of Don Quixote and the Clown, Berger contends that man's ability to laugh at the incongruities of life is yet another assurance that in the depths of his psyche, man feels certain that ultimately all wrongs will be corrected, all evil overcome—there is cause for laughter despite life's many stark experiences. Berger admits, of course, that these five examples of human conduct can be interpreted in other ways, but he prefers to view them cumulatively as pointers to ultimacy.

Response to Ultimate Worth
If there is an ultimate Power behind the universe, this represents only one aspect of the "totally other." For "religious man" also perceives the transcendent as ultimate *Worth*, intrinsic goodness that fascinates and attracts man toward absolute perfection and maximal excellence. That which has appeared to man as a kind of terrifying or tremendous power yet evinces a certain benevolence or goodness, described variously as consummate joy, holiness, light, truth, and life. In short,

5

according to the social scientist, man's perception of the ultimate explanation of life has been that of a life-force that can best be described as a supreme Power-Worth that seems to underlie all reality as experienced by man. In the Judaeo-Christian tradition, this ultimate Power-Worth is called God, conceived as a personal being responsible for man and his worth. It is the Judaeo-Christian conviction that this God, or ultimate Power-Worth, has communicated with his creature man, has revealed himself to him, entered into dialogue with him, and indeed has given of himself to man.

Such a response to this ultimate Power-Worth may well be interpreted as a fundamental "religious impulse" somehow intrinsic to human nature. To the social scientist, this religious response then can be described as a combination of awe-attraction or fear-fascination. Man reverences the ultimate being as supreme power, and at the same time is attracted or bound to this ultimate being perceived as infinite worth and goodness.

NATURE OF WORSHIP

Etymological Insight
Man's religious impulse moves him to attempt to respond to this divine Reality. This response is called *worship*. The word "worship" is derived from the Anglo-Saxon *weorthscipe* (*worth* + *ship*), which means literally an acknowledgement of the supreme *worth* of the ultimate explanation of the universe.[12]

Social-Scientific Definition of Worship
Worship will have many diverse forms, progressing from the near magic rites of primitive peoples, to the liturgy of Christians and Hindus, to the contemplation of the Buddhists seeking Nirvana. Despite such differences, we may essay a common social science defini-

6

tion or description of worship: ". . . the definitive core of all religious tradition, institution, and activity. From worship, all religious life and forms flow as from their source; for worship is the attempt of religious man to hold fast in continuing vitality and availability that Power-Worth experienced at moments of high and intense awareness."[13] Let us now examine this "definition" in greater detail.

Worship as Source of Religious Tradition
From the rather expansive definition given above, it is clear that worship constitutes an essential part of religion. Throughout history, humankind attempted to contact God, especially in ritual celebrations that often included dramatic recitals of divine intervention on humanity's behalf. These interventions in turn were recounted from generation to generation in the form of oral and later written tradition, and thus entered the repertoire of religious ritual. Therefore, worship contributed greatly to the formation of a religious tradition and gradually took a standardized shape or became institutionalized in a relatively permanent, unchanging form. Thus worshipful celebrations help to perpetuate the awareness of the ultimate and the way in which man is constantly summoned to eventual union with the transcendent.

It has always been a challenge to humankind to carry over into daily life the experience of the moments of religious worship. Worship has spurred man to a higher regard for his fellow man, to exemplify in daily life those values solemnly professed at the time of worship. This is what is meant by asserting in the above definition that "religious life and forms flow from worship as from their source."

Worship and Mystical Experience
With the development of the more highly structured religions, the ultimate ground of worship is often the

original experience of the founder—a claimed encounter with the immediacy of "God" without concepts or images (at least in the highest forms of "mystical experience"), or at least an immediate encounter with the transcendent Being that includes a summons or vocation to carry out the mission God wishes to entrust to the founder. In the light of comparative religion, the claimed encounters of Moses or Mohammed or Buddha with the Transcendent have spurred their followers to perpetuate these revelatory events, so that the disciples may share something of the founder's initial experience. The tradition of the Mosaic Covenant of Sinai led to various covenant renewals that helped Israel preserve its consciousness as a people chosen by and bonded to Yahweh (e.g., Deut. 26, Joshua 24). The Christian values highly the messianic consciousness of Jesus and his total devotion to the Father's will leading to the paschal mystery (Jesus' passage through death to a saving resurrection), the cornerstone event of Christian faith. From the social science point of view, a significant purpose of ritual is to answer this need for participation in the foundational encounter.

The social scientist's approach, however, although valid as far as it goes, can only describe and interpret the religious phenomenon of worship. The light of faith takes us to a new level of understanding that the stated parameters of empirical science cannot reach. Therefore, we must now move on to interpret the scientific data described above in the light of the Judaeo-Christian experience of that personal Ultimate Power-Worth we call the God of revelation.

CHRISTIAN VIEW OF THE POWER-WORTH

The Divine Self-Revelation
At the heart of Christian faith lies the conviction that there is indeed a personal God, an infinite Power-

Worth, who has willed to communicate himself to all men and women. This self-communication or revelation can be described as an effort to reach mankind from both the "Without" and the "Within." In a cosmic sense, God reveals himself through the phenomena of nature. Primitive man had a natural reverence for the mystery of nature; the material world around him was charged with an intrinsic sacredness. Fire, water, air, sky, and earth exercised a certain spell over man because they spoke to him of some superior power or force in his life. Paul indicts the Roman "pagans" for a failure to recognize this supernal mystery when he says: "Whatever can be known about God is clear to them; he himself made it so. Since the creation of the world, invisible realities, God's eternal power and divinity, have become visible, recognized through the things he has made . . . . They certainly had knowledge of God, yet they did not glorify him as God or give him thanks" (Rom. 1:19–21).

Interior Revelation
Contemporary thought has tended to accentuate the Creator's will to implant within man an inner awareness of his existence and a consequent impulse to reach out to him. Paul Tillich speaks of God as the "ground of being."[14] In this view, the locus or place of the divine presence is the interior of man. John A. T. Robinson asserts: "God, the unconditional, is to be found only in, with, and under the conditioned relationships of this life: for he is their depth and ultimate significance."[15] Chardin was to maintain: "It is impossible to deny that, deep within ourselves, an 'interior' appears at the heart of beings . . . co-extensive with their Without, there is a Within to things."[16] John H. Wright, building on such insights, asserts: "God acts in the within of all things in the universe. He is present in their within, acting to realize his purpose

everywhere."[17] He notes how the Scriptures speak frequently of God acting upon the "heart" of man, that is, the interior seat of consciousness and feeling and choice. God's action affects the within of each thing, communicating to it existence, being, and reality.

Therefore, God is the source of the reality of all things, as their support of reality and being. He is the attractive impulse, drawing them into the future; he unifies them, ordering them into one universe. He draws our minds and wills to him in love, without compelling us. Thus it is God who first reaches out to us, summons us to an awareness of his presence both within us and in the universe surrounding us. Our quest, then, for the ultimate is not a fruitless one doomed to futility. For the Christian, it is God's self-communication ("grace") to every human being that first calls us to know him, to respond to him, and to be able to reach him in worship both private and corporate.

Dialogical Conception of Providence
Underlying the scheme of God's desire to reveal himself to all mankind and empower them in turn to reach him is a dialogical conception of providence involving basically three moments: divine initiative, human response, and divine response to human response.[18] By our very spiritualness, we feel the "call of the infinite," a sense that we are drawn toward and destined for something or someone beyond ourselves, of a higher order than the corporeal. Created spirit feels drawn to Uncreated Spirit. Divine liberality, infinite graciousness (the Hebrew *hesed*) seeks us out to enrich us and lift us from isolation and alienation to infinite communion with the Transcendent and with one another. This is divine grace.

But we are free beings, endowed with a choice either to respond to this summons to the beyond or to reject it. Openness to God and to others is the response required if we are to receive God's gifts and grow toward the fulfillment he has in mind for us. Confrontation with God within ourselves and with the God who publicly reveals himself in salvation history evokes in turn a continued return-response from God, constantly drawing us to closer union with him into the future Kingdom. The dialogue thus begun by God in nature, through the public revelation to Israel and through his Son, the God-Man Jesus, opens up limitless possibilities for personal and corporate growth within that body or communion that we shall review later in terms of Christ's community, the Church.

CHRISTIAN WORSHIP

As Interior or Mental Acts

Our human response to the divine initiative must perforce engage the inner core of our selfhood if it is to be authentic. Impelled by divine grace, the human mind and will open themselves to God's call from within and respond in the dialogic act called prayer. As Paul assures us (Rom. 8:26), we cannot even begin to "pray" without first being stirred by God's Spirit prompting us to the utterance of praise, admiration, love, contrition, and the desire to have God's fullness replace the void, the emptiness we feel without God. Prayer as an inner gift of self to God is the first stage of worship.

Prayer and Self-Transcendence

To state the above ideas more philosophically, prayer results from a reaching out for absolute Value in a form of self-transcendence, of getting beyond oneself to contact the Eternal. In this process, as Bernard Lonergan describes it, the questing subject moves "from lower to higher levels of consciousness, from the experiential to the intellectual, from the intellectual to the rational, from the rational to the existential."[19] This process of the mind seeks out the ultimate Transcendent, that which "is itself without any conditions whatever; it is formally unconditioned, absolute."[20] Always the Christian recognizes these acts of self-transcendence as a form of grace; the initiative always rests with God.

Once these acts of self-transcendence occur, it is human to express this inward state by acts of prayer or worship. The recognition of a Value beyond human value leads us to love. When that love is the love with which God floods our hearts, we have faith, the "knowledge born of religious love,"[21] which enables us to subordinate all lesser values to the Absolute Value that is Love itself.

Corporeal Worship

Symbol
Worship for man begins then in "spirit," in interior prayer. But we are body as well as spirit; our very God-given nature impels us to express our inner feelings and desires, especially deep-seated feelings such as love, in an external bodily way by signs, gestures, and words that reveal and express our inmost self. We live under the law of symbol.

As body-creatures, we necessarily use signs or symbols to communicate with our world. They may be natural signs like a handshake, a smile, or a kiss; they may be invented signs like a flag, an emblem, or even language. Some signs convey merely a message to my mind, like a price tag on a store item, or a green or red traffic light. Other signs touch me more profoundly when, like the picture of a loved one, they evoke some personal, emotional response associated with the person represented by the sign. Such signs possessing an intrinsic evocative power may preferably be called *symbols*.

The evocative power of symbol is well developed by Avery Dulles, S.J., in an essay exploring the "Symbolic Structure of Revelation."[22] For him, symbol is a special kind of sign, distinguished from a mere indicator (such as a guide's finger) that points to something else, or from a conventional sign such as words. A symbol is "a sign pregnant with a depth of meaning which is evoked rather than explicitly stated."[23] He cites Paul Ricoeur's example of *defilement* in religious literature, used as a symbol for the effects of sin and guilt.[24] Philip Wheelwright's term "tensive" symbol is explained as one that, "draws life from a multiplicity of associations, subtly and for the most part subconsciously interrelated," the kind of symbol that can "tap a vast potential of semantic energy" (quoted on p. 56 by Dulles).

Exemplifying the variety and richness of biblical symbol, Dulles maintains that anything can be a symbol of the divine under favorable circumstances. Among the biblical symbols for God are cosmic objects (the sun, the moon, the wind); particular persons or historical events (Jesus dead and risen, the Exodus); artifacts, like the temple or an icon; and true story, myth, or parable (in other words, various literary forms serving as vehicles for the divine self-communication).

In discussing the singularity of symbolic knowledge, he contrasts it with objective, scientific knowledge. The latter is based on empirical observation plus abstraction from the world about us (cf. the mathematical and exact sciences). However, these do not yield an intimate knowledge of living subjects; our personal knowledge proceeds through an interpretation of signs (gestures, words, etc.) by which people express themselves, and this knowledge of others results in a kind of synthetic, intuitive discernment about them.

Such knowledge through symbols may be called "participatory" knowledge. A symbol is never a sheer object; it opens up a universe of meaning, an "environment to be inhabited," helping us to discover new horizons for life, new values and motivation. Christ's life of obedience, for instance, is the preeminent symbol of his Sonship, which it invites others to share. The Church, the "sign raised up among the nations," is the community of those who are drawn into Christ's way of life and wish to draw others to share this with them. The symbol, then, gives not objective but participatory knowledge.

Further qualities characterize symbolic or participatory knowledge. It may exert a transforming effect upon the knower. It may generate commitment and influence behavior. It stirs the imagination, releases hidden energies in the soul, gives strength and stability to one's personality, and arouses the will to consistent committed action. Witness the power of a flag or anthem to stir patriotism or spark enthusiasm for social and political movements.

Moreover, symbols lead us beyond discursive thought and neat, packaged formulas. They "give rise to thought" by their polyvalent quality. They enable a unification of diverse levels and realities into an integrated view of human existence. Hence for Dulles, symbols are particularly apt for divine revelation that is meant to give us more than mere conceptual information about God. This is because this revelation (especially God's public communication to Israel and through Jesus and the apostles): (1) transforms us into a saving relationship with God ("sons and daughters" of God, friends of God, called to repentance and new life); (2) God's word, in turn, expressed through symbolic revelation, anticipates and stimulates a faith commitment, a total and free trust of ourselves to him; and (3) finally, it gives insight into mysteries beyond reason (e.g., God is both kind and wrathful).

14

One of the most intelligible examples of the rich and varied meanings conveyed by symbol is found in the cross.[25] As a *natural* symbol, it may suggest encounter, crisis, or a moment of choice (crossroads). "Being crossed" evokes collision, opposition. As a wooden object, the cross is a burden to carry. The Romans used it as an instrument of punishment (crucifixion); hence the cross comes to mean condemnation, pain, and death. For Jesus, the cross symbolizes his heroic submission to his Father's will and his unlimited love for us sinners. Other meanings clustering around the cross in salvation history come readily to mind: the Father's loving surrender of his Son as a ransom for us; the enormity of human sin; the agent of reconciliation with God. Liturgically and in Christian art, the empty or jewelled cross points to the triumph of resurrection. For the baptized Christian, finally, the sign of the cross expresses the commitment of discipleship. The cross-symbol, then, has an integrative and reconciling power far greater than any articulate statement or theological proposition. Such evocative power to summon a faith-response is what Dulles means by participatory knowledge.

So far, we have approached "symbol" as an *expressive* and *evocative* function of human and divine communication. But there is another deeper aspect to the nature of symbol that needs to be examined. Not only do we need bodily or external means to express our inner self, but inner realities (ideas, the soul, grace itself) *require* their bodily expression for their own self-realization. The inner reality is *constitutive* of the symbol.

Karl Rahner studies the subject in three sections: (1) the Ontology of Symbolic Reality in General, (2) On the Theology of Symbolic Reality, and (3) the Body as Symbol of Man.[26] We shall limit ourselves to an overview of his articulation of these ideas.

Concerning the ontology of symbolism, he maintains that "all beings" are by their nature symbolic because they necessarily "express" themselves in order to attain their own nature (p. 224). After distinguishing between genuine symbols ("symbolic realities") and arbitrary "signs, signals, or codes" (symbolic representations), he defines a symbol as "that representation which allows the other '*to be there*,' to be actualized" (p. 225). This is the supreme and primal representation.

Being expresses itself because it must *realize itself* through a plurality in unity (p. 229). I take this to mean that intellectual beings such as man must realize themselves in *knowing* and *loving*. These faculties of knowing and loving represent a kind of plurality within man and yet do not really come to function until they are expressed outwardly. "The expression, i.e., the symbol, is the way of knowledge of self, possession of self in general" (p. 230). Furthermore, the figure-forming essence of a being (material, to start with) constitutes and perfects itself by really projecting its visible figure outside itself as its symbol, its appearance, which allows it to be there, which brings it out to existence in the world (p. 231).

In support of his theory, Rahner cites a correspondence with the Thomistic teaching on the *soul* as the animating "form" of the body. In other words, the human soul, at least in its present state in this world, *needs* the body to be fully human. The soul "informs" or vivifies the "prime matter," and the result is a human bodily-spiritual being. Thus Rahner can assert that the body is the *symbolic reality* of man, for the body does not merely point to some other reality. The reality itself becomes real primarily by being *expressed, revealed,* or *symbolized* (p. 247).

"The body is the symbol of the soul, in as much as it is

formed as the self-realization of the soul, though it is not adequately this, and the soul renders itself present and makes its 'appearance' in the body which is distinct from it." (p. 247).

"The symbol *is* the reality, constituted by the thing symbolized as an inner moment of itself, which reveals and proclaims the thing symbolized, being its concrete form of existence" (p. 251).

Applying his theory to the divine plan of salvation, Rahner concludes with a proposition:

"The principle that God's salvific action on man, from its first foundations to its completion, always takes place in such a way that God himself is the reality of salvation, because it is given to man and grasped by him in the symbol, which does not represent an absent and merely promised reality, but exhibits this reality as something present, by means of the symbol formed by it" (p. 245).

Such an assertion permits Rahner to justify the further assertions (to be discussed in the next chapters) that the Church and the sacraments are concrete symbolic realities that "contain" and "make present" what they symbolize.

From the above discussion of symbolic function as *expressive, evocative,* and *constitutive,* it should be apparent that symbolic action is both an apt and most important component of ritual worship, the human response to a loving God revealing himself. It is to this subject that we now turn.

Ritual
Symbolic thinking and acting have been called "consubstantial with human existence."[27] At least in the usage of some experts, *"corporate* symbolic activity" is *ritual.*[28]

Ritual may be conceived, first of all, in a completely neutral sense without any necessary religious connotations. It is an "agreed upon pattern of movement."[29] Children avoiding the cracks in the sidewalk, blowing out candles on a birthday cake, the champagne toast, the more elaborate ceremonials of the Olympics—all of these qualify as ritual in a neutral or secular sense. Anthropologists, too, make much of the initiatory rituals or "rites of passage" that accompany the boundary moments of life; birth, adolescence, marriage, death seem to demand more than a mere passing notice. The ceremonials accompanying these juncture moments of life approach more nearly what we call *religious ritual*, where mankind, primitive or contemporary, confronts the ultimate mystery of the universe and seeks to explain transitional experiences in terms of that mystery. In short, ritual helps us find meaning in the universe and in our own lives.[30]

This illuminative or interpretative function of ritual, as can be seen most readily from the rites of passage, has an eschatological or future-oriented dimension. In every initiatory or transitional ritual, the participant moves from a prior state to a new state of existence (e.g., from childhood to maturity, from the single state to marriage, from death to eternal life). Thus all ritual not only looks to the past (like myth, which reenacts the experiences of the gods) but promises something for the future—ultimately, union with the deity itself. Christian ritual, as will be seen, is always a reenactment of Christ's paschal mystery—his passage from death to resurrected glory—and therefore sets the Christian firmly on the same road to the future Kingdom of the risen Lord, who "makes all things new."

Origin of Rites
Where do rites come from? According to Fr. Bouyer in his study *Rite and Man*, a living rite is not a prefabri-

cated complex of religious ideas put together by sophisticated scholarship; rather "it is an immediate, primordial creation of religiously-minded men in which they have actively realized their effective connection with the divinity before they explain this connection to themselves. This is why at all times and in all places rites are considered to be the work of the gods . . . it is the gods who have instituted them and are the real agents of the rites, working through and beyond the actions of the priests."[31]

These rites, which flow out of man's natural symbolism, are said to be of two basic types, analogous to the sacraments and sacramentals of the Church. The first type is a kind of sacred action that comes from the gods and delivers the divine life itself or blessings from the god to man. The second type includes the ordinary actions of human life, which are brought within the realm of the sacred by divine blessings. In the first type, the actions of the gods descend into the life of man by means of the ritual celebration. In the latter type, our human existence is lifted up into the sphere of the eternal.

Many of the most elementary rituals that underlie the first agrarian civilizations are associated with the theme of creation, an eternal return and a perpetual renewal of all things by returning to the beginning. Other rituals are built around the significance of water. On the one hand water can be destructive, as in the waters of the Deluge, the waters that drowned the Egyptian pursuers of the Israelites, the waters of death in which all the living must finally be swallowed up and perish.[32] On the other hand, water can be creative, constructive, benevolent. In the arid Near East, the need for water to sustain life explains why the sacred authors often use it to symbolize that which is most priceless (e.g., messianic age described by the Hebrew prophets as including abundant rainfall; in the New

Testament, water came to signify the Holy Spirit and the new Christ-life he would bring). Water, too, was thought by many philosophers to be the original medium in which life itself began.

Another ancient ritual is that associated with the meal, in which the taking of food united one with the creative power or served as pilgrim food for the return to the lost paradise. There are also the nuptial and funeral banquets. Such ritual meals underlie much of the significance attached to sacred meals in Judaeo-Christian salvation history.[33]

Sacramental Actions

Ritual or symbolic action, then, is natural to mankind. Rooted in a world already charged with grace (Rahner), human situations, events, persons, and material things have a symbolic value arising out of their divinely grounded nature, prompting the human person to express his deepest spiritual longings, his interior prayer, in a bodily fashion. The human spirit and human love respond to the soundings of the transcendent already present in the world of nature from which primitive man was moved to choose his forms of symbolic expression.

With the onset of public revelation and its focus on the Hebrew nation, human rituals multiplied and increased in complexity. Circumcision, sacrifice, food laws, and feasts came to play a significant role in the way Israel addressed its God.

Finally, with the advent of the Christ and the new Israel, the Christian Church gradually became aware of its vocation to serve human needs and gather up the prayer of the people of God in those dynamic graced events called "sacraments," which built upon the religious sensitivities and experiences of past human history and pointed them to the future newness of the kingdom of God, the "new heavens and a new earth" (2 Pt. 3:13; Rv. 21:1).

Sacramental actions are themselves a profound revelation intelligible only in the Christian context of divine love communicating itself to a world desperately in need of reconciliation and prayerful communion with the heartbeat of the world, which alone can satisfy man's in-built passion for community. It is to this divine-human encounter that we now devote our more detailed attention in the next chapter.

NOTES

1. Wilfred Cantwell Smith, *The Meaning and End of Religion* (New York: Macmillan, 1963), p. 55.

2. Ibid.

3. Ibid., p. 23.

4. For selected examples of such texts, see Winston L. King, *Introduction to Religion* (New York: Harper and Row, 1968); John B. Magee, *Religion and Modern Man* (New York: Harper and Row, 1967); Thomas O'Dea, *The Sociology of Religion* (New York: Prentice-Hall, 1966).

5. King, op. cit., p. 13.

6. Quoted in Magee, op. cit., p. 32.

7. For a more detailed survey of primitive religion and ritual, cf. Magee, op. cit., pp. 41ff; Leonel L. Mitchell, *The Meaning of Ritual* (New York: Paulist Press, 1977), pp. 1–21.

8. Peter Berger, *A Rumor of Angels* (New York: Doubleday, 1969).

9. Ibid., cf. Chapter 3, pp. 61–94.

10. Ibid., p. 78.

11. Ibid., pp. 81ff.

12. King, *op. cit.*, p. 28. For the etymology, cf. *Webster's New International Unabridged Dictionary* (Springfield, Mass.: G. & C. Merriam, 1976), p. 2637.

13. King, op. cit.

14. Paul Tillich, *Systematic Theology* (Chicago: University of Chicago Press, 1951), Vol. 1, p. 235.

15. John A. T. Robinson, *Honest to God* (Philadelphia: Westminster Press, 1963), p. 60.

16. Pierre Teilhard de Chardin, *The Phenomenon of Man*, 2nd ed. (New York: Harper & Row, 1965), p. 56.

17. John H. Wright, *A Theology of Christian Prayer* (New York: Pueblo, 1979), p. 45.

18. Ibid., p. 78; cf. also Karl Rahner, *Foundations of Christian Faith* (New York: Seabury Press, 1978), pp. 116–133.

19. Bernard Lonergan, *Method in Theology* (New York: Herder and Herder, 1972), pp. 34–35

20. Ibid., p. 76.

21. Ibid., p. 115. Since *faith* is a basic concept used frequently in this text, it may be appropriate at this juncture to summarize some of the various nuances of the scriptural use of this word, and then indicate the notion of faith as *virtue* and as *act*, as developed by theological reflection. In the New Testament, the general word for faith is the Greek noun *pistis*; the verb is *pisteuo*. According to R. Bultmann, "The *pistis* Group in the New Testament," in *Theological Dictionary of the New Testament* (Grand Rapids, Mich.: Eerdmans, 1968) (ed. Gerhard Friedrich, trans. Geoffrey Bromiley), Vol. 6, pp. 203–28, *pistis* is the leading term in primitive Christianity for expressing man's relation to God (p. 205). It suggests turning to the God of revelation and accepting the *kerygma* or preaching concerning Christ. Within this broad usage, many specific meanings appear: viz. to *believe* (i.e., accept) God's words (Jn. 2:22; Acts 24:14; Lk. 24:25); to *obey* (Heb. 11; and many Pauline texts); to *trust* or have confidence in; to *hope* (Rom. 4:18; Heb. 11), to be *faithful* (Heb. 12:1). It also involves a basic human *receptivity* to God, actively expressed in obedience (cf. Ernst Käsemann, *Commentary on Romans* [Grand Rapids, Mich.: Eerdmans, 1980], p. 94, commenting on Rom. 3:21). Faith includes a *surrender*, a *personal commitment* to Christ (cf. Bultmann, *op. cit.*, p. 225); it involves

an act of *decision* for Christ as well as the state of persevering in this attachment to the Lord. Always, it is sheer *gift* of God (cf. Jn. 6; Eph. 2:8; Rom. 4).

In theological development, faith was considered a *virtue* or infused (God-given) power to accept divine revelation on God's word alone ("divine faith"), an act especially involving an *intellectual* acceptance of God's word, though ultimately moved by the *will*. Current usage tends to return to biblical sources, and often describes faith existentially as the total surrender of the human person to Christ, which includes accepting the truth of all that He has taught. Throughout this book, I shall try to indicate by equivalent expressions or by *context* what "nuance" of meaning is intended for the word *faith*. (For further reference, consult *The Jerome Biblical Commentary* [Englewood Cliffs, N.J.: Prentice-Hall, 1968], ed. R. E. Brown, Joseph Fitzmyer, and Roland Murphy, esp. pp. 821–22).

22. Avery Dulles, S.J., "Symbolic Structure of Revelation," *Theological Studies* 41 (March 1980) 51–73.

23. Ibid., p. 56.

24. Paul Ricoeur, *The Symbolism of Evil* (Boston: Beacon Press, 1969).

25. Cf. Susanne Langer, *Philosophy in a New Key* (New York: Mentor Books, 1951), pp. 239ff.

26. Karl Rahner, "The Theology of the Symbol," in *Theological Investigations* (Baltimore: Helicon Press, 1966), Vol. 4, pp. 221–252.

27. Mircea Eliade, *Images and Symbols* (New York: Sheed and Ward, 1969), p. 12.

28. Mitchell, *op. cit.*, p. xi.

29. Ibid., p. x.

30. Ibid., p. xiii. For a comprehensive survey of the multifaceted functions of ritual as determined by the behavioristic sciences, cf. George S. Worgul, Jr., *From Magic to Metaphor* (New York: Paulist Press, 1980), pp. 49–105.

31. Louis Bouyer, *Rite and Man* (Notre Dame, Ind.: University of Notre Dame Press, 1963), p. 66; cf. Margaret Mead,

"Ritual Expression of the Cosmic Sense," *Worship* 40: 2 (1966) 66–72.

32. Cf. M. Eliade, *Patterns in Comparative Religion* (New York: Sheed and Ward, 1958), pp. 188ff.; also Mitchell, op. cit., p. 16.

33. Mitchell, op. cit., pp. 17ff.

Chapter Two

The Sacramental Plan of Salvation

THE DIVINE INITIATIVE

In our discussion of the God-man dialogue above
(Chapter 1), it was noted that the Creator-God chose to
initiate a communication with his creatures from both
"without" and "within." Both in the phenomena of
nature and in the depths of man's heart, God reached
out to primitive man, calling him to an awareness of
himself and inviting a reciprocal response from mankind. The human person, in turn, searched the mysteries of the cosmos and sensed an ultimate presence
impelling reverence and fascination, awe and attraction. In this halting way, man sought union with the
Mystery Beyond.

GOD-MAN DIALOGUE DISRUPTED

With the advent of the Hebrew tradition, later incor-
porated in their Scripture, the effort was made to flesh
out something of God's primitive revelation to man.
The sacred authors portray a God raising his creature
to the status of personal friendship, making him divinely lovable by implanting something of godliness
in him. But God's continuing efforts to befriend humanity and lead them to final union and eternal life
with himself (salvation) are thwarted by man's willful
break with God (sin). In the Hebrew tradition, the
widespread contemporary sinfulness present in the
author's times was traceable to a primitive creaturely
revolt against the Supreme Being—a revolt that con-

sisted in man refusing to accept the conditions for
friendship imposed by God. In other words, God had
put man to a test, and man's failure of his test could
have made him an eternal reject. But despite man's
abdication from grace, God's *hesed*, or loving-
kindness, promised to reopen the dialogue of friendship (Gn. 3:15). Somehow the divisive forces of evil
would be conquered; a victory would be at hand for
the human race.

Through the long centuries following the advent of sin
and the consequent rupture in this God-man relationship, man tried to renew the two-way communication
with God, but not too successfully, until God
(*Yahweh*—"I am He who is" or "I am Who I am"; cf.
revelation to Moses, Ex. 3) selected the Hebrews as the
locus for revelation. Ever so gradually, the first "good
news" of salvation (Gn. 3:15) would take shape, as
God selected one man, Abram, and revealed his plan
for reunifying man by the progeny he would raise up
for the patriarch.

THE MEANING OF REVELATION
It was the prideful claim of the Israelites to be the recipients of a special revelation (Latin, *revelatio* "lifting
back the veil"; Greek, *apokalupsis*) by which God
would increasingly make himself known to the people
of his choice, generally through "signs and wonders,"
often announced and interpreted to the community by
mediators such as Abraham, Samuel, the prophets,
and climactically by the Messiah who was to come,
Jesus himself (cf. Heb. 1:1). Gradually, in the course of
this divine "education" of his people, Yahweh revealed something of the "mystery" (*musterion*) of his
identity and of his plan for uniting all humanity to
himself.

The word *musterion* may be traced to the Greek verb
muo, "I close, I shut," originally referring only to the

eyes, ears, and lips.[1] It came to be associated with the secrets revealed only to those initiated into the Greek mystery-cults; the initiate (*mustes*), therefore, was to be a close-mouthed person, forbidden to communicate his hidden knowledge to outsiders. The revealed secret was called *musterion*, and this meaning evidently influenced both the Septuagint[2] and Pauline usage of the term.

Originally, the Septuagint employed the word *musterion* to mean the "secret plan of the king"; later, it took on the meaning of Yahweh's hidden plans for his people and the world. As the revelation of this saving plan developed, Yahweh was seen as showing forth his *wisdom*. Thus as one author points out: "Wisdom and revelation, *sophia kai apokalupsis*, were inseparably linked and correlated to *musterion*. They may be seen in Jewish history and tradition as two beacons piercing the inscrutability of God's way."[3]

THE MYSTERY REVEALED IN THE HEBREW
TRADITIONS—GOD'S SAVING DEEDS FOR ISRAEL
The supreme sign of God's wisdom was his formation of a people who would be a "religious nation," a theocracy, a "sign to the nations" (Is. 11:10), a corporate sign of God's saving presence in the world. In the context of God's grand design to gather this people of God, Yahweh manifested himself from time to time to certain chosen individuals who would further his master plan: to form a people of his own, the community of the End Time.

Signs and wonders, theophanies (appearances of God) became a "normal" intervention of the divine presence. Abraham entertained three mysterious guests at Mamre (Gn. 18), who later in Christian symbolism were often taken to represent the Trinity.[4] The Exodus liberation from Egypt was interpreted as one grand intervention of Yahweh to free his people from Egypt

and form them into a people who would be forerun-
ners of the *ekklesia* of Christ. The pillar of fire, the
cloud, the water, and the desert food were all understood as signs of Yahweh's providential concern for his
people. The Sinai theophany (Ex. 19, 24) most conclusively revealed divine wisdom as Yahweh initiated a
pact with Israel and chose them as his people, obligat-
ed to obey the decalogue code (Ten Commandments)
as their sign of homage and fidelity. From this time
on, he would always accompany them as a "fellow
camper"[5] (cf. Meeting Tent—Ex. 25:8; Nm. 35:34—and
Ark of the Covenant), a presence eventually glorified
in the Solomonic temple, the supreme sign of God's
presence with his people as the personal locus of Israel's national and religious unity.

Yahweh's acts of love toward his people in the first
exodus heartened the faith of Israel and encouraged
hope for the deliverance that came much later when
Israel had been captive in Babylon. The liberation of
538 B.C. marked Yahweh's continuing concern for his
people and, in turn, quickened the expectation for an
even greater gift of freedom in the golden messianic
age that was to come. In this sense, Yahweh's saving
deeds foreshadowed the great redeeming act of love on
the part of his Son made man.

THE MYSTERY AND THE POWER OF GOD'S WORD
Along with Yahweh's *deeds* revealing his presence and
purpose for his people is the scriptural concentration
on the power of God's *word*.[6] While Yahweh revealed
himself mostly by his deeds among and on behalf of
Israel, he is also presented as one whose word is itself
a powerful sign of his actions and his very person.
God is present both as "word" and act.

According to Semitic psychology, man is a totality, a
"one-thing." Thought is also a "one-thing," a total
contact between one's whole being and outside reality.

Therefore, God's thought or wisdom is already an *act* of God's total being. God is present and active, therefore, by his word. The word of God is somehow God himself. In the Hebrew vocabulary, the term for "word" implies action. The Hebrew *dabar* (ordinarily translated "word") meant originally "to push, to go away with, to thrust foward."[7]

Therefore, God's word precedes an event, introduces it, and brings it to fulfillment. For the prophets, God's word is invincible. God "utters a word" (as in the story of creation, Gn. 1) and the word finds instant accomplishment. God spoke and the heavens were made. One of the most memorable prophetic passages illustrating the efficacy of God's word is found in Isaiah 55:10ff.:

"For just as from the heavens the rain and snow come down and do not return there till they have watered the earth, making it fertile and fruitful, giving seed to him who sows and bread to him who eats, so shall my word be that goes forth from my mouth; it shall not return to me void, but shall do my will, achieving the end for which I sent it."

Besides the word *dabar* in the meaning of word-action, the term *memra* was sometimes used as a substitute for God himself, for example in the Targums, the Aramaic translations and paraphrases of the Hebrew Bible. In Genesis 3:8: "They heard the sound of the *memra* walking in the garden." In this latter case, the word is almost identified with God.

All of this Old Testament focus on the efficacy of the divine word prepares us for the sublime title *Logos* ("Word") that the prologue to John's Gospel bestows upon Jesus, the climactic "speech" of the Father to mankind. The Christian sacraments, too, will be seen with greater clarity as Jesus continuing to *speak* and *act* through his Church, the new Israel.

Our dialogic concept of saving history (presented in
Chapter 1) would lead us to expect some *response* on
Israel's part to Yahweh's revelation and wisdom, his
saving outreach to the people of his choice. Israel's
role in the dialogue is a developing ritual of homage
and thanksgiving to its personal covenant partner and
saving benefactor.

In the process, Israel's growing worship patterns
served the twofold purpose of gratefully *remembering*
the past and *reliving* or rendering it ever newly present
as a source of hope for the future achievement of its
ultimate destiny. One of the earliest ritual accounts
appears in Deuteronomy 26:5–10, where the Israelite
farmer is instructed to present himself annually at the
Lord's Sanctuary (Shiloh, Bethel) and offer him the
first fruits of his produce. At the same time, he "remembered" his nation's saving history by reciting a
"cultic credo," a profession of faith and gratitude for
God's mighty Exodus liberation:

"My father was a wandering Aramean who went down
to Egypt with a small household and lived there as an
alien. But there he became a nation great, strong, and
numerous. When the Egyptians maltreated and oppressed us, imposing hard labor upon us, we cried to
the Lord the God of our fathers and he heard our cry
and saw our affliction . . . he brought us out of Egypt
with his strong hand and outstretched arm, with terrifying power, with signs and wonders; and bringing
us into this country, he gave us this land flowing with
milk and honey. Therefore, I have now brought you
the first fruits of the products of the soil which you, O
Lord, have given me."

The Deuteronomist proceeds a bit later to describe a
covenant renewal in words directed to the latter-day
Hebrew:

30

"This day the Lord your God commands *you* to observe these statutes and decrees. Be careful then to observe them with all your heart and with all your soul. Today *you* are making this agreement with the Lord. He is to be your God and you are to walk in his ways and observe his statutes, commandments, and decrees, and to hearken to his voice. And today the Lord is making this agreement with *you*. You are to be a people peculiarly his own as he promised you; and provided you keep all his commandments, he will then raise you high in praise and renown and glory above all other nations he has made, and you will be a people sacred to the Lord, your God, as he promised" (Dt. 26:16–19; emphasis added).

These words of a covenant renewal emphasize that a contemporary of the Deuteronomist (eighth century B.C.?) is just as much a part of the covenant as his ancestors at Sinai. He too is personally involved in the covenant; the repetition of "today" and "you" in the above passage suggests a reenactment of the covenant. Each succeeding generation is personally involved in the covenant with God. The past, so to speak, comes to life in the annual renewal of the alliance with Yahweh. So it was to be in the future. The sacraments of the new covenant would be understood as continuing in a certain way Yahweh's presence with Israel and his saving deeds on their behalf. They were to be experienced and relived by each succeeding generation of Christians as the promise of the ultimate Kingdom Jesus came to establish.

Other ritual acts developed in the course of Israel's history such as circumcision (Gn. 17), an initiation into the covenant; various types of sacrifice and festive commemorations of theophanies and salvation moments (cf. Leviticus); ordination of priests (Aaron and his succession in the Levitical priesthood); sacred meals (e.g. Passover seder, Ex. 12:17 ff.); sacrificial banquets (Lv. 22); and especially with the erection of Solomon's Temple, the development of an impressive liturgy where Israel maintained public, communal contact with its God and responded gratefully to His revelatory love for his people. Over several hundred years, gifted artists composed Israel's hymnody in the form of the psalms—a people's outpouring of every conceivable human emotion (love, reverence, awe, lamentation, sorrow, petition, joy, etc.)—a poetic masterpiece of worshipful dialogue with a tender but demanding Father.

But always in her prayer songs, her sacred meals, her sacrifice, Israel not only remembered and relived the past; she also looked forward to the "fullness of time," the prophetic "golden age," the era of the "new David," the "new Temple," the "new Covenant." Then God's wisdom and revelation would reach its climax, prophecy would reach fulfillment, the messianic age would usher in an unparalleled sign of Yahweh's saving presence, not only for Israel but for all the world. The dawn of New Testament revelation was at hand.

THE FULLNESS OF REVELATION: JESUS
The salvation dialogue of which Israel was a part, as representative of the nations, comes to fruition in the person of Jesus of Nazareth. The former manmade signs of man's reaching out to God (circumcision, sacrifices of animals, purification rituals, Ark of the Covenant, temple) now yield to the perfect symbol of the divine presence—the *God-Man* who is the *symbolic reality* that is signified.

John's prologue expresses this terminal revelation of God to man in terms of language: "The *Logos* (Word, Son of God) became flesh, and pitched his tent among us" (Jn. 1:14). God has spoken and thus revealed the mystery of his wisdom most eloquently in the person of His Son enfleshed as Jesus of Nazareth. Yahweh, acknowledged as "fellow-camper" with Israel under the sign of the Ark in the tent-shrine of the desert, has now come to dwell among men in a new "Tent"—the humanity, the visible bodiliness of His Son. Yahweh, who intended this very image from all eternity, has now in Jesus incarnated that divine Image of Himself, that divine disclosure we call the eternal "Word" of the Father.

In a sense after all we are our language, just as we are our body. Language, whether in words or gesture, is a powerful medium through which we make ourselves known to others. And so it is in Jesus, "the interpreter (revealer) of the Father" (Jn. 1:18), that God is most fully disclosed to us, discovered by us, made accessible to us. "He is the image of the invisible God" (Col. 1:15), "the *musterion* ('mystery') of our religion . . . manifested in the flesh" (1 Tm. 3:16), "God in a human way and man in a divine way."[8]

The New Testament Scriptures leave no doubt, then, that Jesus is the divine *reality* that is symbolized by his *humanity*. John's first letter eloquently expresses the tangibility of God's Son and the validity of apostolic eyewitness of the risen Lord:

"This is what we proclaim to you: what was from the beginning, what we have heard, what we have seen with our eyes, what we have looked upon and our hands have touched—we speak of the word of life. This life became visible; we have seen and bear witness to it, and we proclaim to you the eternal life that was present to the Father and became visible to us. What we have seen and heard we proclaim in turn to you so that you may share life with us. This fellowship of ours is with the Father and with his Son, Jesus Christ" (1 Jn. 1:1–3).

Since the human Jesus is therefore authentically and fully the symbol of the Son of God among men, we may call him as the Fathers often did the "Sacrament" of God, the primordial or core sacrament that not only symbolizes but actualizes the divine presence in the flesh.

By his incarnation or enfleshment, the God-Man became the "Sacrament" or efficacious symbol of our salvation, the revelation of the Father's desire to draw all of us back into union with himself. As Rahner states it, in Christ:

"[T]he whole of mankind is in principle already accepted for salvation in this member and head of mankind who is irrevocably united with God in the unity of person. From the moment the Logos assumed this human nature from out of the unity of mankind, and as a part of it, redemption cannot be arrested or cancelled. The fate of the world has been finally decided, and in the sense of divine mercy."[9]

As the symbol of God for humankind, Jesus is both symbol and cause of God's saving love. His incarnation, life, death, and resurrection are at once the symbol of the Father's saving love and the actualizing cause of this love by being God's acceptance of humankind. Therefore, Jesus represents God reaching out to humankind, and humankind responding to God's offer. He is a living personification of the dialogue of salvation, the embodiment of the *musterion* ("mystery") and divine schema of redemption (cf. 1 Tm. 3:16). As Son of God, he addresses us most authoritatively with the Father's assurance of mercy and grace (*hesed*, "forgiving love"). As man and brother to all of us, he can speak for us the unconditional surrender to the Father's will; he can respond most perfectly to the Father's proffered love by an act of total, worshipful obedience realized ultimately by his sacrificial death on the cross. He is our perfect "yes" to the Father's will, the exemplar of total commitment that the creature owes to its Creator. By this revelatory dialogue, then, he who is perfectly God and perfectly man can most fully "show us the Father," and in turn lead us back to him as the "way, the truth, and the life. No one comes to the Father but through me" (Jn. 14:6). "No one knows the Father but the Son, and anyone to whom the Son wishes to reveal him" (Mt. 11:27).

The revelatory mission of Jesus leads inevitably to his sacrifice of death and resurrection. Mark's Gospel sees him as the Suffering Servant (Is. 53) giving his life as a ransom for the many (Mk. 10:45). John presents him as the true paschal lamb whose blood spares all who believe in him (Jn. 1:29, 19:36). The Letter to the Hebrews shows him as the true high priest of the new creation, who offered not the blood of animals but his own blood, and thus passed into the eternal sanctuary not made by hands (Heb. 9:11–14). Jesus' paschal return to the Father, in turn, confers the promised Spirit who gathers in the messianic community, the new people of God, the Christian church.

THE CHURCH, CONTINUED SYMBOL OF CHRIST'S SAVING PRESENCE

If Christ is the historical symbol of the saving wisdom, the mystery of God's victorious grace extended to all humankind, the church he established is equally an efficacious symbol of his continued presence as Risen Lord heading a new "body" on earth (Eph. 1:22ff.), reaching out to draw all things to the Father (Jn. 11:52, 12:32). The risen Jesus through his Spirit vivifies and unites believing Christians as members of the new people of God (1 Pt. 2:9) on pilgrimage through this world to the Father's Kingdom. Babel is reversed as Pentecost proclaims a new design for unity among men. The Church is the "symbol" held up to the nations, the primordial sacrament of human unity with God.[10] It is not just an empty symbol, however, for

35

Christ's Church as the vehicle of the Spirit is the medium of victorious grace, and is therefore an efficacious symbol of that man-God unity it proclaims and gospels to the world.

It might be well to emphasize at this point that when we speak of the "Church" as symbolizing Christ and making him present as a force for unifying humankind, we are speaking of the Church *comprehensively*— that is, including *all* its baptized members, not just the Pope and bishops (representing the so-called "institutional" model of the church). Vatican II, in its document *Lumen Gentium*, took the same comprehensive approach in the first two chapters, and only in the third chapter ("On the Role of Bishops") did it launch into the institutional model. Chapter 1 ("On the Mystery of the Church") focuses on models like "body of Christ," St. Paul's favorite model, in which the intimate graced union of *all* Christians with Christ the Head is highlighted. Indeed, we are called "the *fullness* of Christ" (Eph. 1:22), extensions of his risen Self, summoned to join him in his worship of the Father and the establishment of his Kingdom on earth.

Chapter 2 of the Vatican document is entitled "On the People of God," once again an all-embracing name for the Church. We are part of a vast community of believers on pilgrimage in this world, headed toward God's ultimate Kingdom, but very much engaged in the Church's contemporary mission of heralding the gospel, building a community of love and justice, and serving the bodily and spiritual needs of the world.[11] We are a Spirit-filled people, guided by him into all truth, with the help of the Pope and bishops who constitute the ultimate teaching authority in the Church.

As baptized Christians, we participate then in the Church's sacramental realization of God's *word*. We are a community that "originates in the word, prolongates the word, and realizes the mission of the word."[12]

Through the power of God's word, we the ecclesial community help to make present the divine offer of salvation which that word signifies. When we proclaim by our witness-bearing the eternal Word that is Jesus, we reflect the innermost nature of the Church as the presence of the risen Lord in history. Obviously, the precise way in which the ministerial priesthood and the baptized Christians carry out this mission of the word will differ by reason of office and charism.[13]

THE CHURCH PROCLAIMS CHRIST THROUGH ITS SACRAMENTAL ACTS

If the nature of the Church is to be a sacrament or efficacious symbol of Christ in the world, it is not surprising that it should carry out its essential activities in a way corresponding to its nature. In other words, it *acts* sacramentally, expresses itself and its saving mission through symbolic acts that continue to present and proclaim the saving Lord to the world and enable humankind to encounter the Christ, who continues to proclaim the Father to us and to lead us to the eschatological Kingdom. In Rahner's words: "The supreme realization of the efficacious word of God, as the coming of the salvific action of God in the radical commitment of the Church (that is, as the Church's own, full actualization), in the situations decisive for the individual's salvation, is the *sacrament* and only the sacrament."[14]

Elaborating on this elemental definition of ritual sacrament as essentially ecclesial, another theologian observes: "As sacrament of Christ, it is the Church that has the vocation of *proclaiming, carrying out,* and *celebrating* the plan of God in each human life and specifically in each major situation of life."[15] Without anticipating in detail the Church's symbolic or sacramental role, which we shall develop later, we may suggest the following. *First,* that in a general sense, all the Church's activities have a certain "sacramental" dimension; she is not confined to ritual acts (the seven sacraments) in pursuing her mission in the world. *Second*, the sacramental activity of the ecclesial community involves both Christ the head and human beings who are both agent and recipient of grace. *Third*, this activity may be envisioned as involving a threefold function: *revelatory*, *actualizing*, and *celebrational*.[16] The actualizing function was discussed during the scholastic period in terms of *causality*: the sacraments "signify" and "cause" grace. In proceeding to analyze what sacraments are, how modern man can better understand their function and purpose, we shall try to give due weight to the other functions of the sacramental Church as well—namely its proclamatory or revelational role and its role of celebration. In the next chapter, then, we shall explore some evidence for "ritual sacraments" in Scripture and attempt to derive a tentative or working "definition" of sacrament by testing the biblical data in accord with later historical, anthropological, and theological developments.

NOTES

1. Cf. Casimir Kucharek, *The Sacramental Mysteries, A Byzantine Approach* (Glendale, N.J.: Alleluia Press, 1976), p. 21.

2. The Septuagint was the Greek translation of the Hebrew Bible at Alexandria, Egypt, traditionally the work of 70 scholars; hence the name *septuagint*, the Latin word for 70.

3. Kucharek, *op. cit.*, p. 39.

4. Cf. the icon of Andrei Rublev, *The Trinity* (15th C. Russian); also mosaic in Church of San Vitale, Ravenna.

5. During Israel's desert journey, the Ark of the Covenant, overshadowed by the cloud of glory, was enshrined in a special tent whenever the Israelites pitched camp. Yahweh was conceived as a "fellow camper," close to his people; hence the word *Shekinah* ("living as in a tent") became synonymous with the "divine presence." Later, John 1:14 would

apply the same image to Jesus, who "pitched a (new) tent" (*eskēnosen*) among men, namely the very flesh of the Son of God.

6. Cf. Alexander Jones, *God's Living Word* (New York: Sheed and Ward, 1961); Carroll Stuhlmueller, "The Sacraments in Scripture," *Studies in Salvation History* (Englewood Cliffs, N.J.: Prentice-Hall, 1964), pp. 128–45; J.L. McKenzie, S.J., "The Word of God," *Myths and Realities* (Milwaukee: Bruce, 1963); Louis Bouyer, *The Word, Church, and Sacraments in Protestantism and Catholicism* (London: Geoffrey Chapman, 1961); Gregory Baum, "Word and Sacrament in the Church," *Thought* 38 (1963) 190–201; Lucien Richard, "The Word and the Sacraments," *Journal of Ecumenical Studies* 2:2 (1965) 234–50.

7. Stuhlmueller, *op. cit.*, p. 136.

8. Edward Schillebeeckx, *Christ, The Sacrament of the Encounter with God* (New York: Sheed and Ward, 1963), p. 14.

9. Karl Rahner, *The Church and the Sacraments* (New York: Herder and Herder, 1962), pp. 14–15.

10. Vatican II, *Lumen Gentium*, par. 1.

11. The reader would do well to consult Avery Dulles, *Models of the Church* (New York: Doubleday, 1974); and John P. Schanz, *Theology of Community* (Washington, D.C.: University of America Press, 1977).

12. George S. Worgul, Jr., *From Magic to Metaphor* (New York: Paulist Press, 1980), p. 135.

13. Karl Rahner, "The Word and the Eucharist," *Theological Investigations* (Baltimore: Helicon Press, 1965), Vol. 4, p. 265.

14. Ibid.

15. Raymond Vaillancourt, *Toward a Renewal of Sacramental Theology*, trans. Matthew J. O'Connell (Collegeville, Minn.: The Liturgical Press, 1979), p. 45.

16. Ibid., p. 91. These functions will be discussed in more detail in succeeding chapters.

Chapter Three

Toward A Definition of Sacrament

We have already noted in Chapter 1, from anthropological and other behavorial-scientific data, man's need for ritual. Ritual, it has been observed, serves a multi-faceted function, including that of helping the individual mature, understand his own identity, and become assimilated into the adult community, accepting the values transmitted from previous generations (socialization). Ritual also serves to remember the past, especially the religious celebration of a so-called charter-event, such as the saving event of Christ's paschal mystery. Moreover, it helps to accomplish and continue community solidarity in a common faith publicly and communally professed. Above all, ritual helps the community and the individual to celebrate the ultimate meaning of human existence and attempt to reach out to and communicate with the Transcendent.

Turning to the Judaeo-Christian tradition (Chapter 2), we have described summarily the faith conviction of Israel and the Christian community that a personal God has indeed progressively revealed himself to mankind. The culmination of this divine disclosure is the climactic revelation of the mystery in the person of the divine Word become flesh—Jesus of Nazareth. We have reviewed briefly the saving Christ-event, crowned with the paschal self-surrender of Jesus in the death, resurrection, ascension, and sending of the Spirit. All of this revelational data assure us that Jesus did not abandon his followers, but that the community he founded is itself mystery—that is, a *saving event*—a sign of his saving activity that we may justly call "sacramental."

THE CHURCH'S COMPREHENSIVE "SACRAMENTAL" ACTIVITY

The ritual activity of the Church must be viewed in the patristic perspective of the Church itself as a "sacramental" reality, a concept that, as we have seen, has been happily recovered by Vatican II and contemporary theology. In other words, the Church, as sacrament or symbol making Christ present in a special way in the world today, may be said to be acting sacramentally in all of its saving mission: (1) the proclamation of the good news of Jesus' death and resurrection as the source of our salvation, (2) the ritual making-present of this saving activity of Jesus in his community today, and (3) the Church's care for human material needs. All of this activity may be called "sacramental" in a broad sense; the Church is constantly acting as a divine-human reality, a symbol of Christ himself still addressing us in our existential situation. It is celebrating his saving work among us, and gathering in the "poor" especially, as a sign of Christ's self-surrender on behalf of all men. It thus reveals the face of a compassionate or loving Christ, trying to make a person and his or her life more human; it leads people into communion with God and their fellow persons, especially in its ritual acts. In all of these activities, the Church is Christ to its members and to the world. It is expressing and realizing its innermost nature as symbol of the Lord's saving presence on earth, therefore acting "sacramentally."

NEW TESTAMENT EVIDENCE FOR RITUAL SACRAMENTS

The primary role of the New Testament community as it functioned to continue Christ's mission seems to have been that of proclaiming the *kerygma*,[1] the "good news" that Jesus who had truly died had been raised up, returned to the Father, and had conferred the Spirit in order to thrust Jesus' followers into their great missionary venture to the world. The apostles and their fellow preachers and catechists not only announced that the eschatological kingdom had arrived in the person of Jesus, but that they, the followers of Jesus, *were* the messianic community, on its way to the kingdom of the End Time. It is within this missionary role of proclaiming God's word that we should locate the ritual communal celebrations now called "sacraments" (cf. Chapter 4). In other words, the gospel "came to life," was actualized, and demanded a faith-response from the hearers in the "sacrament."

We are now in a position to ask: What did the apostolic church do in a ritual way to continue Christ's saving mission? Have we any New Testament evidence for ritual worship in the primitive Christian community? How did they understand their cultic acts, and what was their purpose and function? Can these ritual functions be traced in some way to the will of Christ himself?

In our effort to discover the main outline of what would later be called sacraments in the strict sense, we shall try to avoid a "blueprint" mentality—that is, to expect that Christ himself laid out in specific and explicit details the sacramental rituals as we now know them. As we shall point out later in this chapter, a rigorous interpretation of the New Testament evidence will compel us to take a highly nuanced view of the so-called institution of the sacraments by Christ. Nevertheless, in the case of two sacraments, baptism and eucharist, which have often been labeled by the Protestant Reformers as the two "scriptural" sacraments, we have much more explicit detail than we do concerning any of the other five rituals that eventually

42

came to be accepted by the Catholic Church as con-
stituting sacraments in a restricted sense. Let us now
proceed to examine some of the evidence that the New
Testament provides concerning these two rituals, so
that we may deduce general principles concerning the
nature and function of these two sacraments, and
make some tentative assertions about what Christ and
the Church must have intended for all seven sacraments.

NEW TESTAMENT EVIDENCE FOR BAPTISM[2]
When we search the writings of the New Testament,
we shall find a good deal about the significance of baptism, but little liturgical detail. The New Testament
writings were not intended to give a comprehensive
survey of Church life, but were each written for some
particular purpose and for a particular group of Christians in a given situation. With this reservation in
mind, let us now examine some of the principal allusions to baptism in the New Testament writings to
help flesh out a tentative understanding of that initiatory ceremony that would later be called the *sacrament*
of baptism.

In the Book of Acts, we encounter baptism as the ordinary rite of initiation into the Christian community.
Baptism appears as the *response* to the proclamation of
the gospel. Peter indicates what this response must
be: "Reform and be baptized, each one of you in the
name of Jesus Christ, that your sins may be forgiven:
then you will receive the gift of the Holy Spirit" (Acts
2:38). Constantly, Baptism appears as the rite of initiation into the Church (cf. Acts 8:12–13, 16; 16:31–33;
18:8). The word "baptism," from the Greek *baptizein*,
means "to plunge" or "to immerse." Therefore, it
means essentially to be plunged or immersed in water.
It is of the essence of baptism that it is first of all experienced as an outward ritual, but associated with

this outward ritual is a faith-effect: the forgiveness of sins and the reception of the Holy Spirit (cf. Acts 2:38; 10:47–48; 22:16).

For St. Paul, baptism is essentially Christ-centered. It is into Christ's body that we are baptized (cf. 1 Cor. 12:13; Eph. 4:4–5). We "put on Christ" (Gal. 3:27) at the moment of our baptism. It is Christ's Spirit that we receive in this sacrament (cf. Rom. 8:11, 15). Christ's saving mysteries, his death and resurrection, are re-enacted in us by our immersion into the life-giving waters (cf. Rom. 6:3; Col. 2:12, 20; 3:3).

The synoptic evangelists stress the need for faith to accompany baptism: "The man who believes . . . and accepts baptism will be saved; the man who refuses to believe . . . will be condemned" (Mk. 16:16). The Matthean formula reflects the trinitarian usage of the liturgy of baptism in the Palestinian Church (Mt. 28:19). All three synoptics stress the difference between the baptism of John, son of Zechariah, and the baptism of Jesus, who would baptize with the Holy Spirit (cf. Mk. 1:8; Lk. 3:16; Mt. 3:11). Matthew and Luke add that Jesus would baptize "with fire" (ibid.). Just as the Spirit had appeared at the birth of the world soaring over the waters to make them fruitful (Gn. 1:2), and just as he appeared at the incarnation of the Word forming the body of Jesus in the womb of Mary (Lk. 1:35), so now he appears again at the birth of the Christian, with a purifying action in the soul of the newly baptized as consuming as the action of fire. He takes possession of the person, and for the believer, this is like a new birth that enables him to enter into the Kingdom that John merely foretold.

The first epistle of Peter, which bears many resonances of an ancient initiation rite (e.g. Chap. 2, which speaks of "newborn babes"—probably the newly baptized) stresses the presence of the mysteries of Christ's death and resurrection in the actual baptismal ceremony. "You are now saved by a baptismal bath . . . through the resurrection of Jesus Christ" (1 Pt. 3:21). Baptism makes us priests, "built as an edifice of spirit, into a holy priesthood, offering spiritual sacrifices acceptable to God through Jesus Christ . . . you, however, are a 'chosen race, a royal priesthood, a holy nation, a people he claims for his own'" (1 Pt. 2:5,9). Baptism, too, recalls the blood covenant of Sinai, since by the power of Jesus' blood, the baptized enters the New Covenant and becomes a member of the new Israel (1 Pt. 1:2).[3]

John's Gospel speaks of a new birth "of water and the Spirit" as the necessary condition for entering into God's kingdom (Jn. 3:5). Several of the signs described in John may have a sacramental significance (the cure at the pool of Bethesda, Chap. 5; the healing of the man born blind, Chap. 9; the washing of the feet, Chap. 13).[4] The living waters which Christ promises in his conversation with the Samaritan woman (Chaper 4) are explained in 7:39 as referring to the Holy Spirit who is to be given at Christ's glorification. The living waters flowing from the side of the Savior are fulfilled in 19:34 in the water flowing from the pierced side of Christ on the cross (cf. also Jn. 5:6–8). At this moment, the Spirit issues forth from the crucified and glorified body of Jesus. For one theologian, "at this point and only at this point does Christian baptism become possible. The death of Christ marks the institution of the sacrament."[5]

From this preliminary data, certain highlights about baptism emerge with clarity. Baptism is an outward ritual performed in water, but the baptismal event is more than merely a sign. It causes or brings about an action of the Spirit upon the baptized. It effects the remission of his sins, it joins him to the Christian community, it enables him to become a believer in

Christ. It conforms him to the risen Savior, whose mysteries have a transforming effect upon the inner life of the baptized. Through baptism, Jesus acts by means of his Spirit to impart the fruits of salvation to the recipient. Furthermore, this sacrament of "water and the Spirit" is a ritual performed by representatives of the community of believers. It is a rite of initiation into the Christian body. From it flow all the privileges that accrue to a Christian: fellowship in the breaking of the bread (Acts 2:42, 46), participation in the priestly powers of the community (1 Pt. 2:5–9), and union with Christ in his sufferings and his resurrection (Rom. 6:3ff.; Col. 2:12).

NEW TESTAMENT EVIDENCE FOR THE EUCHARIST
The highest power of the baptized is realized in the celebration of the eucharist, the "Lord's Supper" (1 Cor. 11:20). At this point, we shall merely indicate the chief features of a biblical exegesis of the eucharist, derived from the principal eucharistic texts of the New Testament (the institution accounts in Mk. 14:22–25; Mt. 26:26–29; 1 Cor. 11:23–32; Lk. 22:14–20; and the significant texts of 1 Cor. 10:14–22 and Jn. 6:48–59).

From these accounts, the eucharist emerges clearly as a sacred meal, the chief constituents of which are bread and wine. Behind the external sign of the meal is an event of the metahistorical order: a proclaiming of the death of the Lord (1 Cor. 11:26), fellowship in the Lord's body and blood (1 Cor. 10:16), a new unity among the members of Christ (1 Cor. 10:17), and the celebration of a blood covenant in the very blood of Jesus present under the symbol of wine (all four institution accounts). It is a meal presided over in first instance by Christ himself. It is still designated as his own meal ("the Lord's Supper," 1 Cor. 11:20). It is a meal distinctive of Christian worship, celebrated in the homes of Christians rather than in the temple or the synagogue (cf. Acts 2:46), and demanding faith and charity in the believer (cf. 1 Cor. 11:29; Jn. 6:35, 40, 66). As a meal taken in common, it serves to unite the participants with Christ and with one another or, better, with one another in Christ, all together making up one body (1 Cor. 10:17).

Certain major points evolve from the above survey of the two basic sacraments reported in the New Testament. First, the sacraments are saving events or encounters with the risen Jesus that take place in the context of faith and demand some outward expression of faith.[6] Second, they can be explained satisfactorily only as deriving in some way from the ministry of Christ himself. Third, they are actions of the community, expressing its inner life, contributing to its up-building, and responding to Jesus' revelation of the Kingdom. Fourth, they unite the participant with the dead and risen Christ; they let the Christian share in the great paschal worship of Christ's death and resurrection. Finally, they transform or transfigure the participant into the likeness of the paschal Christ. Putting these elements from the biblical data together, we might then suggest the following as a tentative, descriptive definition of sacrament: *A sacrament is (1) a saving symbolic act (2) arising from the ministry of Christ (3) continued in and through the Church (4) which when celebrated in faith (as adults)[7] joins us to Christ's worship of the Father in his Church and (5) forms us in Christ-likeness, especially in the pattern of the paschal mystery.*

OBSERVATIONS ON A REDEFINITION OF SACRAMENT

Orientations and Purposes of Ritual
It may be observed that our proposed definition corresponds appropriately with the orientations and purposes of ritual described earlier in this text. The ritual acts of the New Testament that we have briefly sur-

47

veyed, namely, baptism and eucharist, are obviously symbolic acts involving initiation into the community (baptism) and a memorializing of the Lord's paschal supper (Eucharist). In both cases, the community is engaged in "remembering" the saving death and resurrection of Christ, his paschal mystery, which is the charter-event upon which their whole life as believers rests. In some way or other, the individual, in being joined to the community in baptism, relives that charter-event; the community itself is sustained by gathering new members. In turn, the community offers the individual who joins it a certain identity, a union with the dead and risen Savior, who in turn is somehow present to lead us into the future Kingdom he has promised.

In the eucharist, that same paschal mystery or crossing from death to new risen life, accomplishing a victory over evil and death, is renewed. The community is nourished with God's word (both in Scripture and in the liturgical retelling of the Last Supper) and his loving act of paschal surrender is renewed under the symbols of bread and wine, which the community would come to interpret as a sacrifice-meal. Again, the charter-event serves as a guaranteed link between the community and its Founder, and also carries on the saving mission entrusted to it by its Head, which is to lead its members and all mankind into the future realization of God's Kingdom. As Paul put it: "Everytime, then, you eat this bread and drink this cup, you proclaim the death of the Lord until he comes" (1 Cor. 11:26).

Theology of the Sacraments
Furthermore our proposed definition includes four elements which illuminate the theology of the sacraments. These elements are (1) that they are symbolic acts, (2) that they have a link with Christ, (3) that they

48

are effective, and (4) that some precise result is effected
by the sacramental act. Furthermore, the definition
also includes three referents; namely Christ, his
Church, and man. Thus christology, ecclesiology, and
anthropology are seen to be closely associated in our
proposed definition. There is no disharmony or dis-
cordance between the anthropological orientations of
humankind, as revealed by the behavioral data we
have briefly touched upon, and the revealed plan of
Christ we have sketched from the New Testament.

Saving Symbolic Act
Our definition contrasts to a certain degree with the
well-known definition of sacrament proposed by the
famous Baltimore catechism of the last century. According to the latter definition, a sacrament was described as an "outward sign, instituted by Christ, to
give grace." Our proposed definition does not negate
the old formulation, but seeks rather to expand and
build upon it in the light of later developments in the
historical, anthropological, and theological sciences.

In using the words "symbolic act" to describe sacraments, we wish to emphasize the contemporary
understanding of symbol. A symbol is indeed a sign,
but yet more potent than other signs. It is super-
charged with a meaning that is not created but discovered by humankind. Symbols reach down to definite
reality; they are ontological in character.

By calling the sacraments symbols or symbolic acts, we
are emphasizing therefore that they are genuine
events, real happenings, "symbolic realities." Symbols
have the power to point to a reality different from
themselves and yet make it present without being
identical with it. In other words, symbols have a direct
and intrinsic relation to the reality they symbolize. To
refer to the sacraments as symbols or symbolic acts,
therefore, in no way diminishes their reality. On the

49

contrary, it points to greater depths of reality and power for sacraments. Sacraments then are not ordinary signs or empty signs, but symbolic realities that bring about what they signify.

Arising from the Ministry of Christ
In both our definition and that of the Baltimore catechism, a link between the sacraments and Jesus is made. Both definitions claim an essential bond between the activity of the historical Jesus and the Church's sacramental acts. The difference lies in the notion of "institution." The Baltimore catechism and the traditional view of sacrament seem to presuppose that Jesus outlined in some detail every one of the seven sacraments. This might be called "blueprint" sacramentology. However, contemporary scholarship finds it difficult to sustain such a literal institution by Christ for each of the seven sacraments. We don't even have in the New Testament an explicit pronouncement by Christ regarding the moment of the institution of baptism, although we do have ample material concerning that sacrament. The origins of the eucharist are clearly traced to the Last Supper. There is certainly a strong hint of Christ's intention that his church should have the power to forgive sins (the conferral of the authority of "binding and loosing" upon Peter and the other Apostles in Mt. 16 and 18, and the power to forgive sins in Jn. 20). Some would also see the origin of holy orders in Christ's mandate of the Last Supper that his disciples should continue a memorial of what he had done there, and this in turn entailed the establishment of the priestly office of offering the sacramental sacrifice. On the other hand, many contemporary scholars would limit direct evidence of Christ's institution of sacraments to those of baptism and the eucharist.

Our problem then is to reconcile the biblical data with that of the Council of Trent and the traditional view of Christ's institution of all the sacraments. Karl Rahner suggests the following theory to explain Christ's institution of the sacraments. He maintains that in establishing a Church that by its nature is sacramental, that is, a symbol of saving grace, Christ willed and intended implicitly that Church to have the power to celebrate those actions that would carry out its fundamental mission of leading men to the Kingdom of God. He puts it this way:

"The fundamental act of the Church in an individual's regard, in situations that are decisive for him, an act which truly involves the nature of the Church as the historical, eschatological presence of redemptive grace, is *ipso facto*, a sacrament, even if it were later that reflection was directed to its sacramental character that follows from its connection with the nature of the Church."[8]

In this view, as in that of many other contemporary scholars, the Church had a definite role to play in evolving specific ritual celebrations in response to the felt needs of man in his existential situation. In continuing Jesus' work of redemption, the Church gradually came to realize that particular communal activities expressed in a heightened form Jesus' saving work. These eventually became known as sacraments. At the fourth Lateran Council in 1215, the number of these activities was limited to seven.

To express the link then with the historical Jesus, we may say that the sacraments "arise from the ministry of Christ"; each sacrament unfolds certain aspects of the Lord's public ministry while he was on earth. The eucharist, the premier Christian sacrament, celebrates the central saving activities of Christ and the core of the Christian faith, namely Jesus' death and resurrection. Baptism and confirmation celebrate the initiation of new members into the Christian community. Reconciliation celebrates Jesus' forgiveness of sin. Matrimony celebrates the intimacy of human love reflecting the love of Christ for his Church (Eph. 5:27). Holy orders celebrates Christ's ministry of service that he demanded of those who are chosen to lead his community. Anointing of the sick celebrates Jesus' healing power. In other words, each sacrament clearly expresses a vital activity of Jesus as Redeemer and Savior sent by the Father to bring about the Kingdom of God in the world. Therefore we may conclude with George Worgul that:

"Each of the sacraments is tied to Jesus, the basic and primordial sacrament. All of the sacraments, and the church itself, arise and flow from the one sacrament of the Father, His only son. The Church, in celebrating the seven sacraments, continues Jesus' ministry. We can then say that in drawing a people to himself, Jesus implicitly "institutes" the sacraments of that people, the church. The church in turn celebrates the various aspects of Jesus' ministry in the various sacraments."[9]

Conclusively then, we speak of the sacraments as "arising from the ministry of Jesus" rather than of their literal institution by him, still insisting on Christ as the originator and final referent of the sacraments, while maintaining the nuances demanded by contemporary biblical, historical, and theological research.

Effectiveness
Both the Baltimore catechism and our definition speak of efficacy attached to the sacraments. Sacraments actually *cause* something to happen. This efficacy must be tied in with the continuation of Christ's ministry in his community of faith, the Church. The scriptural evidence we have brought forth above shows clearly that in the case of baptism, Peter demanded something from those who heard the *kerygma*, namely faith in Jesus' resurrection and a genuine conversion of life, including repentance for sins. In the case of the Last

Supper narratives, there is at least implicitly the demand of Jesus that his disciples believe him when he says "this is my body," "this is my blood"; by accepting the bread and wine that he called his body and blood, the disciples are expressing implicitly their willingness to share in whatever future mission Christ would require. In short, they would be willing to follow him to his passion and death and resurrection even though this is not clear to them at that moment. They are giving their sign of participation in the mystery Jesus is holding out to them under the prophetic sign that we now call the sacrament of the eucharist.

It is clear, then, that on the one hand the rituals of baptism and eucharist we described on the basis of the New Testament data actually caused something to come about by the power of God—the gift of the Spirit and the remission of sins in the case of baptism, and the gift and presence of Christ's sacrificial body and blood in the case of the eucharist. On the other hand, the New Testament data are also clear in affirming the need for a response on the part of the participant. Faith, conversion of life, and commitment to Christ are ways of expressing what is demanded of a person who encounters Christ in the sacramental dialogue.

As sacramental theology gradually took shape with greater explicitness in the later Middle Ages, theologians such as Thomas Aquinas began to speak of two essential and inseparable elements in the sacraments, namely, (1) the action performed, and (2) the attitude of faith in the recipient of the sacraments. *Ex opere operato* and *ex opere operantis* formed one total reality. The *ex opere operato* meant simply what was accomplished by the action of Christ himself in and through the Church. Today we would express this perhaps more appropriately as the outreach of Christ offering himself to us authentically in the sacramental encounter. *Ex opere operantis* expresses both what is demanded for validity on the part of the "doer," that is, the official representative of the Church as presiding over the sacrament, and what is demanded for fruitfulness on the part of the recipient. We speak of this latter under the general heading of "faith," although specific sacraments will require further dispositions (e.g. reconciliation requires genuine contrition, etc. cf. below under "Final Effect"). Sacraments are ultimately fruitful encounters with Christ, then, only when they are received with the proper dispositions. Obviously, we must exclude special cases. What we are considering is the normal case of an individual possessing the use of reason who is called upon to exercise his freedom and total willingness to respond to Christ's offer of salvation.

Of course, we must note in passing that even the faith-response expected of the participant is itself a gift of God. Nevertheless, God waits for the human response of freedom to accept his offer of faith or to reject it. Agreeing with Luther we can say then that God's initiative is preeminent in his dealing with us sacramentally, as in every other aspect of life.

Final Effect
What do the sacraments bring about or cause? As we shall see in later chapters, sacraments were classically understood to confer two effects: (1) that of a closer relationship to the Church (res et sacramentum), and (2) the ultimate effect, grace (res tantum). The first effect was understood as conferring a special relationship with the Church, and furthermore, this effect took place by virtue of the sacramental ritual itself as long as it was done "validly." In other words, the first or intermediate effect of the sacraments included this offer of Christ to be joined more intensively with himself in his community of faith, the Church on earth. But to obtain the maximal effect of the sacraments, namely grace, requires a special disposition or attitude

54

on the part of the participant that will differ with each sacrament. In the case of adult baptism and reconciliation, this disposition includes sincere sorrow for personal sin. In the case of the other sacraments (the so-called sacraments of the living), the general requirement is that of an already existing friendship of Christ (state of grace). Here it is clear that no mere magical approach to sacraments will satisfy; the individual must genuinely enter into the dialogue or encounter by his own faith conviction and practice if the sacrament is to obtain its ultimate or maximum effect.

This effect is usually termed *grace*, or more specifically *sacramental grace*. Every sacrament confers common or sanctifying grace, that is, a general participation in the life of God. Besides that, it was argued, each sacrament must also confer a special kind of grace coinciding with its purpose or function, to enable the individual to carry out the orientation of that given sacrament. Later on, we shall explain in more detail that theological effort to explicate what the specific sacramental graces are.

At this point, it may be appropriate to say a word about grace in general. In scriptural usage, the Greek *charis* ("grace") signifies both the *source* of the gift in him who gives, and the *effect* of the gift in him who receives. The "gift" begins with God's favor, his freely bestowed benevolence. It includes a mingling of tenderness, fidelity, and mercy by which Yahweh defined himself. Yahweh's *charis* is personally revealed in Christ, who is the Father's supreme gift (Jn. 1:17). "God is love" (1 Jn. 4:8); his action is grace (Ti. 2:11).

It is basic to the concept of *charis* as gift that it is *freely* bestowed. The "work of grace" *(charisma)* includes a variety of gifts or charisms (cf. 1 Cor. 12). But fundamental to all such gifts, bestowed for service to others, is grace as a principle of transformation and action, a power that calls for constant collaboration (2 Cor. 1:12, 4:1) and response (Rom. 5:15). It is nothing short of a share in God's own life (Jn. 3:3ff., 5:26, 6:33, 17:2), the life of the Spirit (Rom. 8:14–17).

In Paul, the Christian is "called in grace" (Gal. 1:6), "established in grace" (Rom. 5:2), and lives under its reign (Rom 5:21, 6:14). Grace is life in union with the risen Christ (Rom 6:4, 8, 11, 13) and its results are being freed from sin and sharing the fruits of sanctification-justification worked out by grace (Rom. 3:32ff.).[10]

As theological reflection developed, men such as Augustine grappled with the tension between God's grace as an *influence* upon the human person, his mind and will, and human freedom, which God's grace leaves intact. In other words, somehow, through what came to be called "actual grace" (grace or power for a given *action*), God can impel man toward good without destroying his liberty.

Grace as a principle of transformation, a share in God's life, and the root of powers called "virtues," was designated as *sanctifying grace*. Eastern and Western theology dealt with this supreme gift with different approaches and emphases. Eastern theology took up the more biblical theme that grace is God's presence in man (e.g., Jn. 14:23), that is, the presence of the Three Persons of the Blessed Trinity in the person who is justified or is righteous with God. Thus Eastern theology emphasized a more personal dimension of grace, with God making himself present as to a friend.

Western theology tended to emphasize the other aspect of sanctifying grace, namely, the new capacity that must be created in us in order to accommodate the divine presence. Thus, sanctifying grace was described as a quality created in us to enable us to meet God on a personal basis through faith, hope, and love. The danger of the Western emphasis, however, was that grace would be more readily quantified, that is, treated as though it were a thing that could be measured in amount and intensity. Actually, it is better to think of grace as a relationship with the Blessed Trinity, a relation like other friendships that can grow in various degrees of intensity. Grace then can be understood best by combining Western and Eastern emphases by saying that the Giver comes with the gift. God makes himself present in the person "in the state of grace" and at the same time creates in that person the power he needs to rise above mere human nature and relate more intimately to the divine presence. Thus, to speak of an "increase" of grace is to refer to the growing communion of mind, heart, and will between the individual and God.

CONCLUSION

From what has been said in our efforts to elucidate a tentative definition of sacrament, we have tried to formulate an understanding of this mystery in terms of three referents, namely, Christ, the Church, and man. We have also attempted to show, at least summarily, that the scriptural description of baptism and the eucharist corresponds to the basic ritual needs of man recounted earlier in our discussion of anthropology and the behavioral sciences.

In succeeding chapters, we shall try to elaborate on the various functions of sacraments, grouping them under the rubrics of proclamation, actualization, and celebration.

NOTES

1. *Kerygma* (Greek) means either the "act of proclaiming" (e.g., 1 Cor. 2:4; Ti. 1:3) a message by the *Keryx* (herald or "town-crier") in ancient times, or the "message" itself (cf. 1

Cor. 15:14). In the New Testament vocabulary, the verb form *kerusso* ("to proclaim") occurs 61 times.

2. In English there are presently available several fine works of a biblical and historical nature that study exhaustively the sacrament of baptism in Scripture as well as in the history of the Church. Among these should be mentioned: Rudolf Schnackenburg, *Baptism in the Thought of St. Paul* (New York: Herder & Herder, 1964); A. George, J. Delormé, et al., *Baptism in the New Testament* (Baltimore: Helicon, 1964); Aidan Kavanagh, *The Shape of Baptism*, (New York: Pueblo, 1978); *Made, Not Born* (Notre Dame Press, 1976); G.R. Beasley-Murray, *Baptism in the New Testament* (Grand Rapids, Mich.: Eerdmans, 1962); Jones, Wainwright, Yarnold, *The Study of Liturgy* (New York: Oxford University Press, 1978), pp. 80–85; Casimir Kucharek, *The Sacramental Mysteries, A Byzantine Approach* (Glendale, N.J.: Alleluia Press, 1976).

3. Cf. Carroll Stuhlmueller, C.P., "Baptism: New Life Through The Blood of Jesus," *Worship* 39:4 (1965) 207–17.

4. Cf. Bruce Vawter, C.M. "Johannine Sacramentary," *Theology Digest* 6:1 (1958) 11–16; and Raymond Brown, S.S., "The Johannine Sacramentary," *New Testament Essays* (Milwaukee: Bruce, 1965).

5. Neville Clark, *An Approach to the Theology of the Sacraments* (London: SCM Press, 1958), p. 28.

6. *Faith-context* means that the ultimate reality or event occurs, not on the empirical level, but on the level of God's activity in the supernatural order. Such a happening is knowable only because of divine revelation mediated to us through Scripture and the Church. *Faith-response* involves the expression of the *virtue* or infused *power* to accept God's revelation, especially as communicated in Christ and his deeds, mediated through the Church, and to accept this simply and solely because of God's word (motive of divine faith). Contemporary biblical scholarship also points up the *existential* quality of faith—i.e., faith as a dynamic commitment first to the person of Christ and therefore to all that he teaches. It is generally in this latter sense (faith as *virtuous* response to God) that the word will be used in the following pages.

58

7. By "adults," we mean those having the use of reason and therefore able to respond in faith. Questions such as infant baptism or anointing of an unconscious person are considered distinct cases that need to be treated apart from the normal situation envisioned by the definition.

8. Karl Rahner, *The Church and the Sacraments* (New York: Herder & Herder, 1963), p. 41.

9. George S. Worgul, Jr. "What is a Sacrament?" *U.S. Catholic*, 42 (1977) 30.

10. Cf. Xavier Leon-Dufour, *Dictionary of Biblical Theology*, 2nd ed., trans. P. Joseph Cahill, S.J. (New York: Seabury Press, 1973), pp. 218–20. Also, Ernst Käsemann, *Commentary on Romans* (Grand Rapids, Mich.: Eerdmans, 1980), pp. 153–58.

Chapter Four

The Sacraments as Proclamation

HISTORICAL PERSPECTIVE

In this chapter, we shall discuss the function of sacraments in the perspective of God's word. Word and sacrament have so often been considered disjunctive; the Protestant Reformers, for example, focused primarily on the proclamation of God's word, and the sacraments were considered to be secondary to the Church's preaching mission. It was claimed by the Reformers that God speaks to us primarily through his word, and the Church's mission is principally to continue that proclamation of the divine word. Sacraments, then, are simply another way in which God addresses us, and are therefore subordinate to the overall role of proclaiming the word of God.

The Catholic Church, on the other hand, had come to emphasize sacraments as a cause of salvation; the service or liturgy of the word was considered subordinate and merely preparatory to the essential sacramental act. Hence, a near dichotomy arose between the liturgy of the word and the liturgy of sacrament. A sign of the Church's deemphasis of God's word in the sacramental act was the moral theologians' assessment that the essence of a sacrament was the symbolic act itself. One could satisfy the substance of one's responsibility to "hear" Mass even if he failed to be present at the liturgy of the word, which was considered to be merely a preparatory ritual leading up to the essential act of offertory, consecration, and communion. In the case of other sacraments, a similar downplaying of

God's word was painfully evident. Neither baptism, confirmation, penance, nor anointing of the sick necessarily required a reading from Scripture. Matrimony could be celebrated outside Mass and exclude any explicit Scripture passage, although the "charge" or instruction to the bride and groom was generally a paraphrase of Scripture.

Developments Since Vatican II

In contrast with this earlier practice and teaching, Vatican II has reemphasized the significance of God's word. It introduced the principle that every sacrament must include a liturgy of the word as well as the "essential" sacramental rite, and that somehow these two phases of ritual constitute one single process. No longer is the word considered to be secondary to sacrament; the two must be integrated as one coordinate action of God upon mankind.

In earlier chapters, we have proposed that God's saving design for mankind is essentially a sacramental or symbolic one, that it involves a progressive revelation or proclamation of the divine plan for the world and human beings, present in the mind of God from the beginning and gradually revealed through sacred history until its climax in the person of Jesus. John's Gospel proclaims Christ as the supreme "Word" of God; the Church continues the proclamation of that word and is indeed its living, continuing presence. Sacraments are one means whereby Christ's Church fulfills its mission as the proclamation of God's word and the making present of that saving action that Christ fulfilled when he was on earth; they are a prolongation or extension of his mission of proclaiming the Kingdom and making present its power among men to lead us to the Father and his Kingdom.

Furthermore, we located the revelatory dimension of sacrament within the category of symbolic act. As we proposed in our tentative or working definition of sacraments in the last chapter, they are first of all symbolic acts of Christ arising from his ministry and continued in and through his Church. It will be our purpose in this chapter to examine the possibility that this symbolic activity of Christ continued in his Church is associated somehow with his continued word-encounter with humankind. Sacraments are God's word addressed to us as efficaciously as his word-deeds in past salvation history.

After all, if Jesus is proposed in John's Gospel (Jn. 1:14) as God's Word in the flesh, and the Church is the continued presence and activity of the divine Word made flesh, may we not expect that in some way the saving mission of Jesus is continued as a word-act, especially in those sacred rituals that we call sacraments? Sacraments are celebrations of God's word as his efficacious healing and saving presence among us in and through his Church. After all, God's word has always been a constituent part of the sacramental ritual; what then are the deeper implications of such an association of word and sacrament?

Under the inspiration of a renewed theology of the word, some theologians, such as R. Didier, have tried to synthesize their whole theology of sacraments around the theme of God's word.[1] We might almost say that they have tried to use the theme of God's word as a "model" for understanding the sacraments better. Karl Rahner has asserted that the word of God is primary in the sacramental act.[1a] All of this suggests that new insights may be gained into the nature of sacraments by examining their association with the word of God.

WORD AS SYMBOL

The Word-Component of Sacramental Symbol
From the age of the Fathers through the time of Augustine and Thomas Aquinas, sacraments were viewed as

sacred rituals that pointed to some divine reality beyond. They were symbols of God acting through the human ritual. An essential part of this symbol was a formula of words that were spoken in conjunction with the action. The sacramental ritual may be made up of gestures, words, and sometimes elements such as water, bread and wine, oil, and so on. But in the classical tradition, it was the word that became the determinant factor—it made explicitly clear what the action, with or without the element, really meant. For example, in Matthew 28, which is admittedly of somewhat later derivation than the earlier strata of scriptural material, the apostles are told by Jesus to go, preach to the whole world, and make disciples of all nations, that is, to evoke belief in him and his message and then plunge them into water "in the name of the Father, and of the Son, and of the Holy Spirit." This plunging or baptizing, then, was obviously viewed as a religious act of affiliating the individual with the believing community in the name of the Blessed Trinity. The words make clear that the immersion in water is not an ordinary bath, nor the use of water for some purely human purpose, but a sacred cleansing and an affiliation with the Three Persons of the Trinity. At an earlier stage, apparently the word-formula connected with baptism may simply have been "in the name of the Lord Jesus"; this is an expression often met in Paul's writing. In either case, the spoken word serves to make precisely clear what the external action is all about. Thus it is at the same time a symbol and a cause of the deeper reality that is taking place, the "mystery" or saving action of God upon the individual human being.

The Word-Function in Terms of Sacramental Symbol
When we speak of word as symbol, therefore, we are refining the notion of symbol or sign. As noted in an earlier chapter, a sign may be something static, a mere

object, which when properly interpreted or understood by the onlooker conveys a certain message. Such would be the case with a flag or an emblem. But *word* is a more explicit avenue of communication, a more precise indication of the meaning of a given act. It helps us to understand more directly what the sacramental ritual is all about. Using an image from optics, we may say that the word acts as a kind of lens with which we are able to focus more clearly on what is before us. The sacramental word introduces us to the realm of Christian sacramental symbolism. The word in question becomes the "form" of the sacrament. But it has been suggested that it acts as form not solely at the moment that is called the sacramental rite, but throughout the whole sacramental process (evangelization, catechesis, sacrament itself, and postsacramental catechesis).[2]

The Parameters of Sacramental Sign Language
Furthermore, sacramental symbolic language, like all languages, uses symbols that have their context in a given culture. This raises the problem of the universality of language, its regionalization and its evolution. We know that at a given period in their history, certain words become freighted with more meaning and emotional connotation. Christian symbols are no exception to this phenomenon of acculturation. They must therefore be reevaulated in the light of their deeper meaning. The liturgical renewal of Vatican II has confirmed the need for such an effort.

Therefore, viewing the sacraments as word-symbols highlights them as a kind of sign language. Obviously, if the sign language is to be effective and communicative, it must be intelligible; otherwise no dialogue is possible. This is why Vatican II reintroduced the vernacular language into the liturgy, and also simplified and revised the sacramental rituals so that their meaning would be understood more readily by all participants in the sacramental action. Unless Christ's gesture of saving love is clear to us, how can we make an appropriate response, individually and communally, in a way that is natural and meaningful to us?

The Sacramental Word and Realism
Finally, word as symbol in reference to sacramentality has a note of actuality or realism, about it. This is confirmed in different ways.

First, such realism attached to the sacramental word is justified phenomenologically when we reflect that the person in the symbol or the word reveals himself and is therefore in a sense "present." We express and actualize our inward self in an external way through our body, through symbols—words, gestures, body language, or whatever. We reflect and express ourselves outwardly in the symbol, especially the word that we utter. If the symbol or word is authentic, it will express honestly the person who utters it; if the symbol is inauthentic, the person is still revealed in that symbol, but as one who is dishonest, masking the true self. Applying this to the sacramental word, then, it is defensible to maintain that the word of Christ, uttered in and through the Church, must actually involve the presence and saving activity of the Word made man; he is ultimately speaking and acting through his body and symbol, the Church.

Furthermore, we must recall the Hebrew notion of God's word as "event," suggested by the word *dabar* (as explained in Chapter 2). God's word accomplishes what it speaks about; therefore, it is not an empty utterance, but a reality (cf. Is. 55). Karl Rahner comments that a sacrament is a specific word-event. Word is essential; the words of Christ make the sacrament. The matter or material element is secondary; it serves to

clarify the word. Rahner reminds us that two sacraments, matrimony and reconciliation, do not have a
material element such as water, oil, or bread and wine,
but only words. This would seem to support his insistence on the primacy of word in the sacrament. Christ
at the sacramental moment is present in his word. Paul
reminds us that it is the word of God that proclaims
the Lord's death in the eucharist (1 Cor. 11).[3] God's
word, in short, is grace-event, salvation-event; it leads
us into the long line of salvation history.

THE SACRAMENTAL WORD AND SALVATION HISTORY

The "Sacramental" Word and Israel

Salvation history, as revealed in the Scriptures and in
oral and written tradition, is the inspired record of
God's actions among men with a view to bringing
them into community with himself. Our study of the
Hebrew traditions shows us God's word revealing his
wisdom and eternal mystery, his plan regarding Israel
as a bridgehead for reaching all mankind. He revealed
himself not only in words, but in deeds that served to
reveal the face of God to the Hebrew nation, to reveal
the kind of God he was, and to enlighten them as to
his mission or plan for Israel as a light or a sign to the
nations. The supreme revelation in the Old Testament
came to light in the form of the Exodus, the great act of
liberation in which God not only freed the Israelite
tribes from Egypt but made them his own people, to
be mediators to the rest of the world.

Christ, Sacramental Word of the Father

The fullness of the revelation of the mystery came in
the person of Jesus as the very Word of God in human
flesh. In terms of Christian revelation, especially as
John's Gospel presents it, we can say that Jesus is the
true sacrament of the Father's presence among men.

Jesus is God's very Son, the image of the Father spoken and revealed to men most clearly and explicitly in the human nature of the God-Man. He is the supreme revealer of the Father, showing us what God is like and at the same time proclaiming the ultimate Kingdom of God, which Jesus has come to inaugurate and bring to fulfillment. Therefore, Jesus is the definitive Word of God, the sacrament par excellence of the Father.

The Church as Sacramental Word of Christ
The Church in turn, is likewise a symbol of the divine Word made flesh in Jesus. It continues the speech-event of Christ's saving work. It is charged with revealing to others the mystery of God made man and what that mystery entails, namely, the in-gathering of all people, Jews and Gentiles, into the one Kingdom of God. The Church is Christ's herald, charged with the office of proclaiming Jesus as Messiah and Risen Lord who has opened the way for all men to return to the Father. The heart of the good news is that Jesus, who has nailed sin to the cross, has been raised up and thereby conquered sin and death for all humankind. Little wonder then that the Church's essential mission should be presented in the New Testament as "proclamation"; its missionary activity takes precedence over all its other roles. The Church's chief mission is to reveal the divine Word incarnate in Jesus of Nazareth. The Church herself as the living symbol of this divine Word makes Jesus present and continually active in all his healing and saving deeds among men. It does this in various ways by preaching, by healing, by celebrating the sacraments, by its works of charity, and by its outreach of love.

Sacraments as Word-Events
If the Church is essentially herald of God's Word revealed in Christ, we may in turn expect the sacraments

to be word-events in the life of the Church community. The sacraments are closely tied in with the *kerygma*, the good news. When Peter proclaims the good news of Christ's resurrection (Acts 2:38) and his listeners question him as to what they must do to make up for causing Christ's death, he answers that they must change their life (be converted) and receive baptism. Thus the ritual of initiation into the community through plunging in water in the name of Christ or the Trinity becomes an outward and communal sign of one's acceptance of the gospel and one's commitment to live according to that gospel. In Matthew 28, as we have seen, the final charge of Jesus to his disciples is phrased in terms of their preaching the good news, eliciting faith, and then sacramentally baptizing the believer in the name of the Blessed Trinity. Thus the sacramental ritual, as we now call it, serves to fortify one's adherence to the gospel and functions as an external ritual of admission to the community of believers in Christ.

Even more pointedly, Paul associates the *kerygma* with the eucharist. In I Corinthians 11:26, he asserts that whenever Christians eat the body of Christ and drink his blood, they are "proclaiming the death of the Lord until he comes." The word "proclaim" here is the verbal form of the Greek noun *kerygma*; in other words he is saying "whenever you celebrate the eucharist you are 'gospeling' the death of the Lord until he comes." Thus the intimate association is most clearly established between the proclamation of the *kerygma* (the Lord's passover mystery) and the sacramental proclamation of one's identification with the *kerygma*.

We are reminded that the sacramental word is spoken by the entire Church, Head and members acting together. Clearly the visible Church cannot itself confer the grace of salvation. Only Christ can definitively lead us to the Father through death and resurrection, through those symbols that make that charter-event of salvation present and active throughout history. Therefore the Church's sacramental word is also the word of Christ, for here she is acting in her specifically saving role of gathering in the followers of Jesus, catechizing them, and calling them to a deeper faith in Christ as Savior.

THEOLOGICAL DEVELOPMENT OF SACRAMENT AS THE SAVING WORD OF CHRIST

Patristic Phase
The writings of the Fathers of the Church who describe the sacramental practice of those early centuries attribute great importance to proclamation or revelation as a dynamic factor in the sacramental process. The ecclesial communities of the time were very conscious of their vocation to reveal to Christians the many aspects of the mystery of salvation. The sacramental celebrations were a major part of the pedagogical and evangelical vocation of the early Church. In the case of Christian initiation, which was sometimes spread out over several years, the Fathers had a rich opportunity to proclaim the mystery of Christ as revealed in the rituals of the sacraments. Furthermore, at the various stages of human life, the early Church communities aided their members in discovering aspects of God as well as the full meaning available to the human person in a given life situation.

If we take St. Augustine as a kind of spokesman for the end of the early period of patristic tradition, we cannot fail to note his famous expression concerning sacraments that when "the word is added to the element we have a sacrament."[4] The "word" here is understood as a symbol of Christ's direct participation in the sacramental act. It is a definitve statement that what is taking place is an event of the divine order, not merely an empty ceremonial, edifying though it may be.

Medieval Shift

The earlier function of the sacraments as revelatory of the mystery of salvation ceased to be a primary concern once the Church had taken root in the Western world; it became less preoccupied with revealing its own mystery than with showing Christians all the implications of a mystery with which they were assumed to be already familiar. In this phase of the Church's life, from the Middle Ages to our own day, emphasis came to be put on another function of the sacraments, namely making something actual or real. At the time of Aquinas (1224–1274), sacramental ritual came to be analyzed in more philosophic language. Thomas divided sacramental ritual into *matter* and *form*. (This may or may not have been a conscious adaptation of Aristotelian physics.) Thomas said that the matter of the sacraments consisted of the action performed and the element, if there was one. The form of the sacraments consisted of the words that accompanied the ritual celebrations. For him, the form was decisive in making the ritual abundantly clear. It was Thomas who, in his theologizing about sacraments, placed them under the category of sign. At the same time, he distinguished sharply between sign and causality. For him, the sacraments are not merely empty signs, but actually cause what they signify. Nevertheless, a kind of dichotomy or split could be anticipated as a result of such theologizing. Gradually, more emphasis came to be placed on the causal power of the sacraments and less on the word-power to evoke sacramental meaning and faith. Abuses crept in that led to an almost magical or mechanical use of sacraments as rituals that took effect *ex opere operato* (from the action itself that was performed), independently of the response of the participant.[5]

Reformation to the Present

Such an accentuation of the *power* of the sacraments at the expense of the *proclamation* value of the ritual was bound to evoke a negative response from the Reformers. The latter, under the leadership of Luther, tended to follow the Augustinian stress on the power of God's word. According to the Reformers, God's word is addressed to us in two ways: through Scripture and preaching on the one hand, and through the sacrament on the other. But God's major initiative toward us occurs through the word of revelation, which in turn demands a faith-assent on our part. To the Reformers, without this latter response the sacramental act is meaningless. Thus a cleavage between what we now call the liturgy of the word and the liturgy of the sacraments developed. As we noted earlier, the Reformers emphasized the power of God's word and tended to diminish the importance of sacraments by contending that the sacraments were simply another way in which God speaks to us. The Catholic Church continued to emphasize the power of the sacramental action and tended to diminish the importance of God's word. The word-service came to be looked upon merely as a preparation, a kind of stimulus or mood-setter, for the really important action: the sacramental act itself. It remained for contemporary times, under the leadership of Vatican II especially, to work toward a unity of word and sacrament, a balance, an integration of God's outreach to man in the symbol of his word and the symbol of the ritual action.

CONTEMPORARY ATTEMPTS AT INTEGRATION OF WORD AND SACRAMENT

Current Influences

Many factors contributed to restoring the significance of God's word to a place of honor in the celebration of the sacraments: the study of the sources, a better knowledge of the history of sacramental practice, and also a consciousness of the current reality that Christians are facing a new type of hostility in a world sometimes called "post-Christian."

On the other hand, the preaching of the primitive Church, as well as during the great periods of missionary activity, was directed to a world in which natural religion was a major factor in life. This is no longer the case. Sacramental practice has been profoundly affected in the process; sacraments are no longer being viewed by some authors as a form of worship that is owed to God, but as a sign of membership in a social group that is differentiated from the bulk of mankind.[6] A sacramental celebration, then, must have as one of its functions to make explicit the purposes that motivate its participants and make them different from others. The pastoral approach to the sacraments must foster an awareness of the specific meaning of Christian life.

Sacramental Word as Revelatory
In light of this felt need for greater emphasis on the sacraments as motivational and pastoral, we may ask: "How is the relation between word and sacrament in continuity with the Christian tradition?" The study of the origin and history of our word "sacrament," and of the reality it has designated in the course of centuries, relates it to the Greek word *musterion* used by St. Paul. For Paul, the term signified the secret plan of God as revealed by his Son, the man Jesus. This unique *musterion* was prefigured in the Old Covenant and is experienced in Christian liturgical celebrations. In the latter case, the Fathers spoke of *musteria* (the plural form of *musterion*)—the "mysteries."

The Latin translation of the Bible came to use the word *sacramenta* to designate the "mysteries" celebrated in Christian worship. This does not mean to restrict the word "sacrament" only to liturgical rites. But it does include these, mainly to the extent that they reveal, make real, and celebrate the events that accomplished our salvation in Christ. In other words, in the original use of our word "sacrament," the aspect of manifestation, revelation, or epiphany took priority over the aspect of instrumentality, rite, and causality. Fr. Yves Congar, often called the world's greatest living Catholic ecclesiologist, has summarized the work done on the history of this word *sacramentum* and its relation to the Greek *musterion* as follows: "We may therefore assert that the role of the word in the sacraments is essential. It is essential in respect of the rite itself, according to the well-known statement of St. Augustine that was to be constantly repeated later on: 'the word is added to the element, and the result is a sacrament.' The words in question are not just any words but words that likewise refer to God's plan of salvation and to the Covenant; they are therefore words which act as a memorial that actualizes the saving intervention of God and the mystery (mysteries) of Christ. The words in this case are not simply cognitive, not simply the expression of ideas and sentiments, but are in their own proper way a communication of the reality or actualization of it that reaches its completion in the celebration of this reality."[7]

Sacraments as Speech-Acts
Current interest in the philosophic analysis of language and its structure and meaning provides still another approach that, in effect, serves to unite or integrate "word" and "sacrament." Several theories have been proposed to interpret Christian sacraments by viewing them as *speech-acts*, or a unique type of religious language.[8] I have chosen to present a brief overview of only two of these theories that seem to serve our present purpose best.

Sacraments as Unique "Limit" Language
The first theory deals with the subject of *religious language* and how it can serve to mediate the meaning of Christian sacraments.[9] The author (William M. Shea) begins by tracing various levels of questioning and showing that ultimately one reaches certain boundaries or *limits* that necessitate moving to another level for an "answer." Each level has its own language of discourse. For example, the scientist can attempt to reach certain conclusions or truths by the empirical method of experiment and investigation. But if he asks: "How is scientific knowledge possible?" or "What is it about us and our universe that allows scientists to raise and answer questions?" he has moved to another plane of discourse, namely the philosophic; on this level he must follow the procedures, the structures, and employ the language of philosophy, not science. He has reached a limit on the strictly scientific level and must adopt a different approach when he wishes to deal with ultimates that transcend the empirical method.

Likewise, the philosopher (e.g., an ethician or moralist) who asks "Why be good or truthful at all?" or "How can we explain the human drive to value and truth?" ultimately reaches a limit where he may have to resort to symbolic or analogical language and refer to the Unmoved Mover, First Cause, Absolute Spirit, and so on. He arrives, in short, at the boundaries of "religious language."

Besides the limits to scientific and moral discourse and the various philosophic attempts to deal with "limit-questions," there are also "limit-experiences" or "limit-situations." These are moments within ordinary secular experience that appear extraordinary, but are not overtly religious. They lead one to experience the meaning of one's life as finite and self-transcending.

Negative experiences such as one's life being broken

74

by guilt or sickness, or the emptiness and fragility of one's life prompting anxiety about death, may push one to the limits of ordinary experience and evoke questions of a more ultimate nature. Positive experiences, too, such as joy and peace that seem beyond explanation in the face of enormous suffering, the experience of loving and being loved, the sense that life is after all worthwhile and to be cherished—such positive experiences may be inexplicable in ordinary terms. Ordinary and literal language breaks down; we sense that something is beyond.

It is at this point that religious language enters, the "primary language of the limits. It meets dread (as in the case of negative experiences) and allows faith."[10] It deals with the "horror and beauty of what we call 'God.'"[11]

Religious language is metaphorical, symbolic, and poetic. It attempts to express the Transcendent in story, myth, parable, poetry, and proverb. It is the peculiar human response to limits experienced in mind and heart; it provides a language for the ineffable.

Christian language is one among many religious languages; its distinctive character lies in its assertion that "Jesus is the Christ." In this credo is expressed the uniqueness of Christian meaning. In spite of our sin, God will not leave us alone. What he did for Jesus (especially the resurrection), he will do also for us.

This meaning comes to its clearest existential expression in Christian *worship* and *sacraments*. They are "the primary Christian limit-language"[12] and the immediate experiential source of Christian religious language. The sacraments are celebrated especially in the limit-situations from birth to death, from loving to sin.

Sacraments mediate or express the limits of the expertise of the participants. As a community language, they allay the anxiety of finite existence and celebrate the joy of God's gift of eternal life. In common we share a past, present, and future. "In Adam we have all sinned; in the Eucharist we are all one body; in Christ is our hope of glory."[13]

Sacraments, then, are mediated to us through the Church, whose language and meaning is discovered neatly in its worship. The Church conceives itself as speaking for the Transcendent. This so-called "Catholic" principle of mediation not only corresponds most aptly with man's nature as historical, social, and psychological being, but also involves a certain infallible efficacy. In classical terms, this means that the sacraments confer the *res et sacramentum* (like the "character" or seal of baptism) and in turn make the *res tantum* (sacramental grace) available to man.

In conclusion, this theory of sacraments as speech-acts regards them both as man's language about God and human language by which God speaks effectively to man. They speak, in short both *of* the limit and *from* the limit!

Three "Languages" of Sacraments
The second theory recognizes that the liturgy of Christian sacraments is itself a language that speaks and conveys meaning. Hence the emphasis of this theory is on the linguistic structure of sacraments as evidenced in the liturgical texts and ritual performances.[14] This theory maintains that there are "three languages" discoverable in Christian sacraments.

The first language is that of human dynamics; each sacrament is a *genuine human event* constituted by action and interaction that have meaning in themselves. For example, the eucharist is first of all a shared meal. (Therefore, it should look like it and "behave" like it.) Initiation is a welcoming into the community. Marriage is a public expression of love and commitment

76

between two people. This language matrix is the most important in sacramental worship, in the sense that what it does or does not "speak" determines the success or failure of the other languages involved. It is the language of space, movement, and interaction and is prior to the "word" proclaimed upon it.

The second language (the "word," the language of proclamation and explanation) along with the first constitutes an action as *sacrament*. The word articulates the deeper meaning of the action, namely, God's gracious (though invisible) activity and presence. It is the language of song, prayer, and proclamation that announces the faith-meaning of the event. It is evocative, inviting, only indirectly instructional, speaks *to* God, and seeks the community consent or commitment, "Amen." Among the many forms of proclamation in a given sacramental ritual, one is a *privileged* form: the core of the eucharist, for instance, is the great prayer of blessing, the eucharistic prayer including a double invocation of the Holy Spirit upon the gifts and for the unity of the people. It is on this level that the liturgy most aptly draws upon the symbolic resources of a people's culture in order to reach the whole person: intellect, will, and emotions.

The third language is the *reflective* language of theology (including catechetical language and liturgical commentary). It is declarative, directly instructional, and seeks the response "I understand." Theology must speak its truth back into the worship event itself; it must be translated into the language of movement and proclamation (e.g., turning the altar toward the people as a sign of the meal aspect of the eucharist, or the restoration of the epiclesis or invocation of the Holy Spirit in the "proclaiming" prayer, the result of theological reflection on the role of the Holy Spirit). Surely it was the theological data (as well as knowledge derived from the historical and behavioral sciences) that inspired many of the ritual revisions of Vatican II.

The author concludes with a pastoral observation that is well-taken. There must be no conflict between the first two languages. He cites a cartoon from the *Critic* that depicted priest, deacon, and subdeacon dressed in classic black funeral garb. They looked with sober scowls as the smoke of incense enshrouded the coffin. The caption spoke the word proclaimed on this event: "I am the resurrection and the life." Obviously the two languages of event and word were not harmonious.

The merit of this language theory applied to sacraments may be succinctly stated in the author's own contention that the *entire* liturgical event becomes equally as important as what earlier tradition called the *essence* of the sacrament. Sacramental adequacy means more than essentials. The complex language of ritual must address the believer properly, and the believer in turn must be properly prepared for and open to what the ritual speaks and accomplishes. Such an integrated worship truly unites word and sacrament and invites reflection on its evangelizing potential, to which we now turn.

EVANGELIZATION AND SACRAMENTS

Interrelationship
In examining the current theological interest in sacraments as proclamation, or to put it another way, the interrelationship between word and sacrament, we must not fail to observe the consistency of Vatican II in reemphasizing the importance of God's word in the sacramental ritual (e.g., giving us a richer diet of Scripture over a three-year cycle, stressing the homily, etc.) and also insisting on the Church's mission of evangelization or heralding the gospel. The Council, which put great stress on this in its document on *The*

Church in the Modern World, finds an echo in the words of Pope Paul VI. In his *Apostolic Exhortation on Evangelization*, for example, he wrote:

"Evangelization therefore reveals its full potentiality when it establishes a close link, or rather an unbroken continuity, between word and sacrament. Ambiguity is the result when, as sometimes happens, an opposition is set up between the preaching of the Gospel and the administration of the sacraments. Undeniably, of course, to administer the sacraments without having given solid catechetical instruction on them or even without any general catechesis is to deprive the sacraments in large measure of their effectiveness. The duty of the evangelist is to educate men in the faith so that each Christian will be induced to live the sacraments as authentic sacraments of faith instead of receiving them passively or even unwillingly."[15]

Some theologians go so far as to say that we must not place the Church's proclamation of the word and the celebration of the sacraments on an equal theoretical plane. Primacy and priority must be given to the proclamation of the word.

"One cannot, strictly speaking, say that the saving activity of the Church includes the proclamation of the Word and the use of signs. Rather, the proclamation of the Word is the activity of the Church that includes everything else. Even the use of the signs is fundamentally a saving preaching of the Word for two reasons: First, because it is only the Word together with the thing that constitutes the sacramental sign, with the Word having the chief importance; secondly, however, because the significance of the sign itself is proclamation."[16]

The same author goes on to say: "The use of signs is part of the Church's task in preaching the word, not vice versa."[17]

It should be noted, however, that the sacraments have a unique place among all other proclamations. In the course of its mission, the Church legitimately proclaims many things in contemporary language, which is therefore marked by a certain variability. But in sacraments, the ecclesial words express the very essence of the Church. In sacraments, the word of the Church is the proclamation of the word of God that signifies and effects salvation.

The kerygmatic power of the sacramental word is brought out finally in depth by Karl Rahner when he comments on the primacy of the Church's spoken word in the sacrament over the "matter" used in the sacramental ritual. It is only the spoken word, he maintains, as an expression of human transcendence, that allows the possibility of God's self-communication within sacramental celebrations. The supernatural reality of God acting through the Church can display itself only through the medium of the human word because of the basic spiritual, transcendental openness or orientation of man pointing beyond the finite to God himself. Thus man acting and speaking in the name of the Church becomes an intrinsically constitutive element of the sacramental sign. The sacramental minister, in other words, speaking and acting in the name of the Church, is himself acting as a medium or vehicle of evangelical proclamation.[18]

The Sacramental Process
Along these lines, Vaillancourt extends the notion of the sacramental process in terms of proclamation by asking whether we should not consider much of the preparation for sacraments as part of the celebration itself. In other words, we limit too narrowly the notion of sacrament to the moment of celebration. Should we not go further and speak simply of the sacrament as including the entire pastoral approach to sacrament,

including the preparation, in which the word plays such a large role? Here we think, for example, of the restored rite of the adult catechumenate, in which time plays such an important factor; that is, the time required for the true conversion of the candidate before enrollment in the Church. The same thing may be seen in the case of the sacrament of reconciliation, in which the sacramental celebration as such is viewed as a kind of end product of a process in which the sinner asking for forgiveness has already made a sincere effort at interior conversion of life.[19]

WHAT EXACTLY DO THE SACRAMENTS PROCLAIM OR REVEAL?[20]

We may approach this subject from a twofold point of view: thematically or topically, and temporally. In comparison with the Baltimore catechism definition of sacraments as "signs of grace," the present explanation may seem somewhat complex. Nevertheless, it aims to be more comprehensive and more explicit.

Topically or thematically speaking, we may say that the sacraments reveal the actions of Christ, the Church, and man. Temporally, as Thomas Aquinas said so long ago, sacraments signify and reveal a threefold time dimension. They are related to the *past*, they signify and cause something to happen in the *present*, and they also promise or guarantee something for the *future*.[21]

Proclamation of the Paschal Mystery

First, in terms of Christ, sacraments proclaim and reveal the saving actions of Christ during his ministry on earth, and in a climactic way, they manifest the paschal mystery, the "root-metaphor" or charter-event upon which all Christianity rests. Thomas Aquinas teaches that the sacraments derive their power from the passion and death of Jesus.[22] We would say today that they get their power from the whole paschal mystery, including the death, resurrection, and sending of the Spirit. In some way or other, each sacrament reveals and proclaims the whole death-resurrection experience of Jesus, the historical personage on earth. His death-resurrection event is the source of all the power of the Church and the sacraments. In some way or other, that power is symbolized, revealed, proclaimed, and made present in each and every one of the Church's sacramental acts. It is the *mystery* of Christ, the creative word of God revealed, made present, and actualized among men.

If the death-resurrection experience or the paschal mystery of Christ is the source of our salvation, each sacrament in one way or another proclaims and reveals the presence of that mystery or saving event for our benefit in a given situation of our life. As Paul explains in Romans 6, baptism by immersion is an especially vivid demonstration of our being plunged into the death of Christ (through immersion into the water—a sign of drowning our past sins), rising from the baptismal pool becomes a sign of our joining Christ in his new risen state. Reconciliation is likewise death to sin and resurrection to a new union with Christ. Matrimony means "dying" to one's solitary and often self-centered existence and rising to a new life for others (spouse and children).

Each sacrament, insofar as it arises from the public ministry of Jesus, may be said to reflect a certain aspect of that ministry. For example, the sacrament of reconciliation reflects Jesus' forgiveness of sinners. The sacrament of the eucharist reminds us of Jesus' feeding the crowds with his teaching and the promise that he would feed us with his own flesh and blood (in the eucharist). His healing works are continued in the sacrament of healing, the anointing of the sick. His concern for human love, evidenced at the miracle of Cana, may be said to be reflected in the sacrament of matrimony. Thus each sacrament reveals a certain facet or aspect of Christ's public ministry on earth. It links us then with the public ministry of Jesus and also with his death-resurrection. The sacraments are definite ties with the past historical deeds of Christ on earth.

Proclamation of a Present Encounter with Christ
But each sacrament, as Aquinas reminds us, also signifies, and therefore effects, some affiliation with Christ in the present moment.[23] At this point, we are concerned with the revelatory feature of the sacramental act. In the present moment, the sacrament reveals Christ's present activity *in and throughout the Church*. For it is only through the Church, the extension of his Incarnate Word, the fullness of his risen body, that Christ can continue to act upon us and with us today in the sacraments. Sacramental symbol, therefore, proclaims the action of the Church as the word of Christ continually spoken among us. We are enlisted in the great lineage of salvation history—God's saving acts in the past continued and made present through his sacramental deeds in the Church. Past and present coalesce as the Church continues to celebrate among us and to make efficacious for us the saving deeds of its Founder and Head.

The sacraments, however, do more than reveal the Church in its ministerial function. Since in its fullest comprehension, the Church includes all the baptized faithful, we are all involved in the sacraments; therefore, every sacramental celebration in one way or another reveals and makes present the acts of the whole Church. Every sacramental assembly is a primary sign of the whole Church at work and at worship, professing its belief and expressing the creativity of the faith community.

The entire assembly, Head and members, realizes in

the present moment and proclaims its vocation of inserting us into the saving paschal mystery of Christ in the different situations of our life: birth and maturity, sickness, marriage, and the time of death. The Church is at our side as the body of Christ directing us toward the ultimate source of meaning and strength. Thus the whole assembly of believers discovers sacramentally its vocation of being one with us at the juncture moments of Christian life.

Proclamation of the Future Kingdom

Sacramental signification and proclamation is not confined to the past and present. It propels us also to the future Kingdom proclaimed by Christ, present in him, and yet not fully realized.

As Aquinas put it, the sacraments are a guarantee of immortality. They show us the immortal, risen, and glorified Christ as the model and image of what we all are to become. They also spur us on to become individually transformed Christians while on earth, daily taking up our cross in the hope and assurance that this imitation of the Suffering Servant will help to transform us one day into the glorified and triumphant servant of the Lord.

Furthermore, sacraments coincide with anthropological orientation. They not only reveal to us *who we are*, but help us discover what it means to be truly human and point the way to *what we are to become* as fulfilled Christians. They help make our human existence more meaningful, heighten our human dignity, emphasize our position as sons and daughters of God, and looking ahead to the future, show us what we are to become—sketching for us glorified Christians made in the image and likeness of the risen Christ, human persons who will have overcome the limitations and barriers of sin and death, and who are transformed as members of the mature risen and glorified Head.

In this way, we can see that the sacraments signify, reveal, and proclaim Christ, the Church, and humankind in the threefold time dimension of past, present, and future. This complex role of sacramental revelation should not dismay us, but rather enhance our appreciation of Christ's "being-with-us" in and through the Church's ritual proclamation.

THE SACRAMENTS AS DIALOGUE OF FAITH

Word and Dialogue

Up to this point, we have considered the sacraments primarily as Christ's and the ministerial Church's proclamations, without reflecting much on our expected response. If we move from the model of proclamation or revelation to the model of dialogue or encounter, then the sacraments appear as ecclesial celebrations of our dialogue with Christ in the Spirit, a *response* to Jesus' revelation of the Father's love.

Scriptural Perspective

Our personal involvement in the sacramental encounter may be described as that of faith and total openness to God.[24] That we are to come to the sacraments with faith can be seen from the fact that in Scripture, salvation is attributed sometimes to baptism and sometimes to faith, as though one or the other were all-sufficient. Actually, the one includes the other; baptism for adults presumes an act of supernatural faith on the part of the petitioner. Baptism, in other words, is itself an act of faith. In John 3:5, the new birth of water and the Spirit is proclaimed as a prerequisite for entrance into God's kingdom. In Romans 6:3–14 and Titus 3:5, the same insistence on baptism is again apparent. In John 3:36 and Romans 10:9, faith alone is mentioned as the gateway to salvation. "Whoever believes in the Son has life eternal. Whoever disobeys the Son will not see life, but must endure the wrath of God" (Jn. 3:36). Romans 10:9 puts it this way: "For if you confess with your lips that Jesus is Lord, and believe in your heart that God raised him from the dead, you will be saved."

The nexus between faith and salvation appears frequently in the Gospel miracles of Christ, which are figures or signs of his ongoing healing power among men. In many cases, Christ first demanded faith in him, or at least in his power, before he would work a miracle (cf. the cure of the paralytic, Mk. 2:1–12; the hemorrhaging woman, Mk. 5:25–34; the raising of the daughter of Jairus, Mk. 5:22–43; the cure of the daughter of the Syro-Phoenician woman, Mk. 7:24–30). It would follow logically that the sacramental celebrations of Christ's healing power likewise demand faith from us if they are to attain their full effectiveness in us.

Even this response of faith to the healing word-action of Christ is not wholly of our making. The initiative comes from Christ's grace, which moves us to respond freely to his offered gift. We are not justified, we are not sanctified without our cooperation. We are saved as free, responsible persons. God does not force his gifts upon us against our will.

Dialogue as "Offer" and "Response"
The saving event (proclamation, revelation) that occurs in the sacraments may be said to include an offer and a response. The "offer" is the self-communication (word) of God toward man; the divine saving presence of Christ through his Church in the sacramental encounter; and the accessibility or availability of Christ in his passover mystery to draw us into union with his Father by the influx of his Holy Spirit. Such a loving gesture is but an extension of the revelation of God toward Israel, and toward all humankind in the incar-

86

nation of his Son and in the Church. Through the incarnation, the divine Word appeared on earth as Jesus of Nazareth, who became the living sign of God's presence among men, divinity made visible in the flesh. The Church as Christ's word and God's image continues God's presence among men in Christ. She is "the sign set up before all nations" of the continuing presence and proclamation of Christ. The sacramental celebrations, then, are privileged moments when this saving word of Jesus in his Church becomes supremely actual for us, when his saving love and grace reach out to us in terms of a personal and communal encounter.

The response phase of God's saving work is likewise grounded in New Testament salvation history. Christ, the divine Person made man, returned to the Father as the perfect servant of the Lord in his act of total dedication and love (Is. 53:10; Mk. 10:45). The Church as Christ's body must also be consciously attached to her Head by loving devotion. As his bride bound to him in love (Eph. 5:25f.), she participates in this gesture of loyal commitment to the Savior. In every sacrament, therefore, besides God's movement toward us by his offer of saving grace (often called the *opus operatum* of the sacrament), there must also be the response of man through the individual and corporate prayer or confession of faith expressed in the liturgy of the sacraments; in other words, man's faith and loving commitment must be given freely in conscious and willing acceptance of God's offer of grace in the sacramental encounter (the *opus operantis* of the sacrament). It is in the context of the *opus operantis* that the place of faith in the sacraments must be elaborated.

Symbols of the Faith of the Church[25]
The ecclesial dimension of every sacrament is apparent in that the institutional Church determines the real

meaning of the sacramental rite. Any religious symbol receives its significance from the religious community in which it is employed. This also occurred in the Church under the guidance of the Holy Spirit, as the Church through the centuries developed a suitable matrix of rite and gesture in which to locate the central sacramental act of sanctification willed by Christ. Through the objects used (water, bread, wine, and oil), the gestures performed, and the words that accompanied such gestures, the Church came to express her faith in the purpose for which each sacrament was willed by Christ. Thus a study of this outward symbol, the symbolic rite of each sacrament, will reveal to us the ultimate purpose of the sacrament according to the belief of the Church.

Especially in the sacramental words (called by Aquinas the *form* of the sacrament), the Church determines more precisely the ultimate meaning of the various religious symbols. Little wonder that the Fathers of the Church call the sacramental word the "word of faith." By her word of faith, the entire Church receives the saving mercy of God proceeding from the Father in the Son, through the power of the Holy Spirit. Through the liturgical prayers of the sacrament, the Church expresses the transcendent meaning and the present reality of the sacrament, its divine power and content.

Sacraments are not automation, nor are they magic by which we capture for ourselves something of God's power. Sacramental salvation is *received* from God, not created by us. We must not participate in this saving event like robots, computer operators, or vending-machine patrons, mechanically obtaining "cheap" grace by performing certain required motions. Rather, sacraments touch the heart and core of human existence; they demand a total self-donation in response to the unutterable gift of God in Jesus Christ and the Spirit.

Symbols of Faith on the Part of the Participant
Since the sacraments are community celebrations, they
are first of all expressions of the faith of the whole
Church, but in addition to this communal expression
of faith, each Christian must make a conscious adherence to Christ as an active member of the faithful. For
the Christian filled with faith, this means that he looks
beyond the mere externals of the sacramental symbols
and sees there the action of Christ. Baptism is not
merely a bathing of the body; it is identification with
the saving death-resurrection of Christ. The eucharist
is not just bodily nourishment; it is a sacrifice-meal
with the risen Christ, at which his glorified flesh and
blood nourish the believing worshiper and join him
more fully to the believing community.

Not only does the believing Christian approach the
sacraments with the *vision* of faith, looking beyond the
external ritual to the encounter with Christ that occurs
there; the believer must also come to the sacraments
with the *commitment* of faith. Faith is more than an intellectual grasp of a supernatural reality; it is the surrender of the whole personality to Jesus the God-Man,
present and active in the sacramental experience. This
surrender engages one's will; it demands the gift of
oneself, total service, a whole-hearted dedication, the
surrender of all that is deepest in one's being, a total
response to Christ's outreach to us.

It is this kind of faith, stimulated by individual acts of
God's "elevating" grace, that enables the adult
catechumen to pledge himself unreservedly to a faithful and obedient Christian life. It is this kind of faith
that enables the confirmed Christian to consecrate
himself courageously and steadfastly to the mission of
bearing public witness to Christ in every area of his
life. It is this kind of faith that the Christian community and each individual Christian offer to God in
every eucharist by means of the bread and wine. It is

this kind of committed faith that the believing Christian brings to the sacred meal of the eucharist when he receives Christ and pledges his "Amen," as though to say "I adore, I praise, I love you, I want you, I surrender myself to your service." Only if the Christian brings this kind of committed faith to his sacramental encounter with Christ will the power of the sacraments in turn influence his daily life. Only with this kind of faith will the Christian's life become transformed gradually into Christ.

Encounter in Christ with such wholehearted surrender will surely cause the faithful member of God's people to grow into a deeper, more intimate faith in Christ and in the Father. Indeed, Vatican II assures us of the power of the sacraments to stimulate faith in the worshiper:

"[The sacraments] not only presuppose faith, but by words and objects they also nourish, strengthen, and express it; that is why they are called "sacraments of faith." They have indeed the power to impart grace, but, in addition, the very act of celebrating them effectively disposes the faithful to receive this grace fruitfully, to worship God duly and to love each other mutually" (CSL, para. 59).

THE SACRAMENTAL WORD AND LITURGICAL RENEWAL

Objectives of the Renewal: Clarity of Symbol
In the light of the foregoing, it is not difficult to see why the ritual of the sacrament, at least in its main outlines, should be clear to the faithful (CSL, para. 59, 62). "It is of the greatest importance that the faithful should easily understand the sacramental signs" (CSL 59). The Council also mandated the revision of the sacramental rituals to update them according to contemporary needs (CSL 62). The easier it is for the Christian

to understand the meaning and relevance of the sacramental proclamation, the more readily he can respond to the mystery with full faith and participate actively in the celebration.

One of the primary considerations for liturgical participation is that of language. If the sacramental rite is a kind of dialogue between God and man, how can I take part in such a dialogue if I don't even understand the language that is addressed to me? A sacrament is addressed not only to God but also to the celebrating participant. The early Church felt this and used the vernacular language in every instance for several centuries. It was only when the Western Mass became ossified in Latin about the ninth century that the linguistic barrier, which still prevailed into modern times, was first erected. Vatican II restored to the faithful the privilege of the mother tongue in the liturgy of the Mass, the sacraments, and the sacramentals (CSL 63). On the other hand, as liturgiologists and other experts have noted, religious symbols (e.g., the altar, the cross, the baptismal font, the paschal candle, the very elements used in the sacramental rituals such as bread, wine, oil, water, etc.) have many layers of meaning (*multivalence*), whose richness is not to be depleted or overlooked by an oversimplified ritual. To put it another way, liturgy proclaims the ineffable mystery of God and our relationship to him. It should, therefore, be celebrated in such a way that our daily lived experiences are taken up into the transcendent, are given a new meaning, and are "informed" by the ritual celebration of the Infinite. In short, ritual should not only speak to us intelligently, but should also convey a sense of wonder and awe as we confront the hidden majesty of the Divine.

Cultural Adaptation
In the sacramental liturgy, the actions should also reflect local cultures (CSL 63b). Diverse cultures may ex-

press identical religious sentiments in highly different ways. It is not uncommon, for example, for Asiatic and African peoples to express intense religious emotion by means of a sacred dance (cf. 2 Sm. 6, where David danced before the Ark of the Covenant as it was being escorted in triumph to Jerusalem). Western gestures such as the imposition of hands, which occurs in the baptismal service as a gesture of acceptance by the Church, may have a totally different meaning in a different culture. In the Orient, for a man publicly to place his hand on the head of a woman is regarded as a proposal of marriage. If the sacramental symbol of ritual, then, is to be authentic and faith-stirring, it must make sense to the assembled faithful and must be intelligible to them; it must be in harmony with the cultural understanding of the people for whom it is intended as a vehicle of worship.

Esthetics of Celebration and Proclamation
The nobility of worship invites beauty of expression; liturgical celebration ideally should be a "work of art." It should inspire, uplift, and edify the celebrating community. Along these lines, Susanne Langer's concept of the "art symbol" may have appropriate resonances here.[26] According to Langer, the art symbol is the work of art itself as an image or articulation of feeling (p. 125). It is an "expressive form" (p. 134) that formulates an "import" rather than a meaning. "The work as a whole is the image of feeling, which may be called the Art Symbol."[27] It articulates feeling in a beautiful and integral form.

Applying this to liturgical celebration, we do not mean to imply that it should be a purely emotional experience. But as a work of art or "art symbol," it should evince a concern for perfection of form and for holistic appeal, including the sensual or emotional. The artistry of the celebration (including the "presidential" manner, the music, the environment, the assembly's role) should present the sacramental *symbol* so as to highlight its importance and significance. In other words, it must *impress* the participants with a sense of the sacred, manifested in a context of beauty; it must express the profound significance of the mystery being enacted. It will thereby contribute to the total efficacy of the celebration, that is, in evoking a more intense response of faith by the entire assembly.

Robert W. Hovda, long concerned with the art and power of sacramental celebration, could remark about its efficacy:

"The power of acting out in rite that divine dominion to which we have assented but which is in constant tension with the structures and institutions by which we operate and live—that power is . . . immensely more effective in communicating the reality of God's dominion than any number of theological books, or retreats, or moral exhortations, etc. . . . Whatever can be done to make that liturgical experience more real, more participative, more communicative, *more beautiful*, more involving, is apt to be more effective for the good news than most of our other ecclesial activities."[28]

Biblical Awareness
Besides the concerns for clarity, native cultures, and esthetics, yet another consideration is involved in the liturgical proclamation. As the Church evolved the ritual for her sacraments she drew heavily from the treasures of Sacred Scripture. The sacraments, after all, are deeply rooted in salvation history; hence, the outward form of the sacraments proclaims the saving act of God in evocative biblical terms. The water of baptism, for example, is meant to recall not only the priceless value of water for the people of the Near East in our Lord's time, but also its association with saving history. The ancient practice of baptism by immersion

93

more vividly portrayed the Christian's association with Christ's burial and resurrection; the contemporary practice of baptism by infusion (pouring the water over the head) less obviously expresses the deepest significance of the sacrament. From this it follows that our people need an intensified biblical orientation. The better they know Scripture, the more they will come to appreciate the message of sacramental celebration. Biblical instruction becomes a kind of stepping-stone to the faith; that is, to be moved by the sacraments, the faithful should have an elementary grasp of salvation history. With this they will come better prepared to the sacramental encounter with Christ, and they will come away from it not only united more firmly with Christ, but also better instructed in the tenets of the faith. The liturgy then becomes, as it was in the early Church, a school of learning, for it was in the liturgical assembly, the synaxis, the proclamation of God's word, that the catechumens received their basic orientation in the faith.

Tension between the Sacred and the Secular
Current commentators on liturgy articulate a curious tension between a desacralization of liturgy on the one hand and a preservation of the sense of mystery on the other. By desacralization, they seem to mean that liturgy must make contact with the reality of our world as we experience it. A liturgy for dockworkers, common laborers, the intelligentsia, children, must be adapted to the intelligence, the concerns, and the interests of each group. It must make contact with human reality. On the other hand, liturgy must not be eviscerated to the point that we lose all sense of the sacred, the Transcendent. We do not come to the worship celebration as we do a party, a dinner meeting, or a labor union meeting; we come for a communal faith-filled encounter with the Divine. Somehow, future implementation of liturgical modifications must strive

for a happy balance between the two poles of human experience: our human environment or our daily life on the one hand, and our desire to enter into communion with the sacred on the other.

FAITH AND FRUITION

The intensity of faith and love that we bring to the sacraments will also affect the total efficacy of God's word addressed to us in the sacraments. If all the requirements are met for a true sacramental celebration (validity), then Christ actually offers us himself and his saving grace in the sacramental word-encounter. The sacrament achieves a certain efficacy already from this very fact (e.g. imparting of the sacramental seal in baptism, confirmation, and orders; the sacrifice of the sacramental body and blood of Christ in the eucharist; the spiritual bond in marriage). The maximal effect of the sacraments—actual union with Christ through his Spirit, a sharing in his life and his love, the actualization of new life in us—requires on our part a real advance toward Christ in a loving commitment of loyal faith. Once more, then, the importance of the sacramental proclamation in evoking and expressing our response in faith is verified.

NOTES

1. R. Didier, *L'Eucharistie, le sens des sacraments*. (Lyons, 1971), pp. 166–71, 300–14.

1a. Karl Rahner, "The Word and the Eucharist," *Theological Investigations*, Vol. 4 (Baltimore: Helicon, 1965), p. 266.

2. Cf. Raymond Vaillancourt, *Toward a Renewal of Sacramental Theology*, trans. Matthew J. O'Connell (Collegeville, Minn.: The Liturgical Press, 1979), pp. 71, 95–96.

3. Rahner, op. cit., p. 267.

4. St. Augustine (*In Joannis Evangelium*, 80,3: PL 35, 1840).

5. Among such abuses might be mentioned the attitude to-

ward the Mass as a "good work" that we merely have to attend; Mass without communion of the faithful; excessive concern for Masses for the Dead; multiplication of Masses to satisfy the stipends offered; a kind of "laundromat" approach to penance, where the priest's absolution was regarded with more concern than the penitent's sincere contrition and conversion.

6. Vaillancourt, *op. cit.*, p. 93. In my own view, there should be a balance between sacraments as worship and as catalysts of community.

7. Yves Congar, *Un peuple messianique*, Cogitatio fidei, # 85 (Paris: Le Cerf, 1975), p. 53.

8. Cf. A. Martinich, "Sacraments and Speech Acts," *Heythrop Journal* 16 (1975) 289–303, 405–17; Wm. M. Shea, "Sacraments and Meaning," *American Ecclesiastical Review* 169:6, (1975) 403–16; Peter E. Fink, "Three Languages of Christian Sacraments," *Worship* 52 (1978) 561–75. For philosophic background, cf. Paul Ricoeur, "The Hermeneutics of Symbol and Philosophical Reflection," *International Philosophical Quarterly* 2:2 (1962) 191–218. Also by the same author, *Freud and Philosophy: An Essay on Interpretation*, trans. Dennis Savage (New Haven: Yale University Press, 1970), 3–56, 344–551.

9. William M. Shea, op. cit., 403–16.

10. Ibid., p. 407.

11. Ibid.

12. Ibid., p. 408.

13. Ibid.

14. Peter E. Fink, *op. cit.*, 561–75; for the importance of the liturgical text as theological source, cf. David Power, *Ministers of Christ and His Church* (London: Chapman, 1969).

15. Paul VI, *Evangelii Nuntiandi*, #47, trans. in *The Pope Speaks*, Vol. 21, (1976), p. 25.

16. Michael Schmaus, *The Church as Sacrament*, Dogma 5 (London: Sheed & Ward, 1975), p. 17.

17. Ibid.

18. Rahner, op. cit., p. 267.

19. Vaillancourt, op. cit., pp. 95–96.

20. It is difficult to avoid a certain overlapping with the next chapter on "actualization", since what the sacraments proclaim or "symbolize" they also "cause", objectively speaking.

21. S.T., III, 60, 3.

22. S.T., III, 62, 5.

23. S.T. III, 60, 3.

24. Cf. above discussion of concept of *faith* on p. 22, footnote 21.)

25. Cf. Bernard Cooke, *Ministry to Word and Sacraments* (Philadelphia: Fortress Press, 1976), p. 645.

26. Susanne K. Langer, *Problems of Art* (New York: Scribner's, 1957), esp. Chap. 9, "The Art Symbol and the Symbol in Art," pp. 124–39.

27. Ibid.

28. Robert W. Hovda, "Liturgy as Kingdom Play," *Worship* 56:3 (1982) 263. Emphasis added.

Chapter Five

The Sacraments as Actualization

In an age of computerization and sophisticated
technology when so much of human behavior is pro-
grammed for us, there is a danger of expecting the
same kind of mechanical efficiency in our relationship
with God through the Church and the sacraments.
Technology has made it possible for us to control space
satellites with astounding accuracy and efficiency. Automation makes food and drink available at the drop of
a coin. Rapid change makes us impatient with the
status quo and expectant of immediate results for a
minimal investment of time and energy. If this mentality is transferred to the realm of sacraments, we may
unwittingly come to think of them as dispensers of
easy, packaged grace. All we have to do is carry out
the prescribed ritual of words and actions and infallible results will follow. Of course, this is a travesty
of the orthodox doctrine on sacraments as encounters
with the risen Christ, as celebrations of his paschal
mystery, that challenge us to live out the same death-
resurrection mystery in our daily lives.

A healthy corrective to a *quid pro quo* outlook on how
sacraments work and what they accomplish will be to
examine pertinent biblical and doctrinal formulations
and attempt to correlate this data with contemporary
philosophic and social science insights. It is to this
task that we now turn.

In the previous chapter, we have discussed the revelatory or proclamatory function of sacraments—sacraments as a kind of sign language in which Christ addresses us, proclaims his saving love for us, reaches out to us as the Father's definitive word of healing, expressing the divine will to gather us together as the messianic people destined for the Father's Kingdom, a kind of nucleus of all humankind's destiny to be united in community with the Trinity. The emphasis rested on the model of sacraments as a *word*-function, announcing through the Church Christ's revelatory mission to acquaint us with the Father in and through the Spirit.

The present chapter accents the sacraments as *actualizing* events, brought about by the sacramental word "spoken" by Christ in and through the Church. Our study will show the further unfolding of the sacraments' revelatory dimension, delving more deeply into the word-*event* already suggested by the rich meaning of the Hebrew term *dabar* ("speech-event"). We will examine the sacraments as much more than isolated "rites." Such rites, when taken out of context, can lead to the danger of being interpreted and used in an almost magical or at best merely mechanical way. We shall view the sacraments in their total context as actions of *Christ*, the *Church*, and *man*, and compare this approach with Scholastic discussions on the efficacy or causality of the sacramental symbols.

We shall not only maintain that the sacraments genuinely re-present Christ's paschal mystery of death-resurrection, but shall also indicate the latter's potentially transforming effects upon the sacramental participants. If the sacraments are "made for man" as the Scholastics maintained, we will show how they are directed to the whole person, not just toward revealing

99

a message to the intellect, but toward effecting a thorough change in human life. They exercise a "humanizing" as well as a "divinizing" function—helping a person to be more authentically human as well as more genuinely Christian.[1]

PHENOMENOLOGY AND ACTUALIZATION
Before commencing an historical review of the Church's understanding of the actualizing function of sacraments, we will observe how the contemporary philosophic approach called "phenomenology" helps us locate our study in terms of the interaction between *person* and *symbol*. An awareness of this contemporary insight will help affirm the traditional view of sacramental efficacy, and at the same time better prepare us to correlate the "sign of the times" with traditional doctrinal formulations.

The Approach of Phenomenology
Phenomenology as a philosophic approach to reality is generally ascribed to the German philosopher Edmund Husserl, who wanted to analyze the data of human experience as accurately as possible to reach the "primitive fact" underlying the human situation. His process involves two stages: (1) *describing* the phenomenon as a "lived experience," viewing it in its fullest possible context so as ultimately to understand the meaning of the phenomenon; (2) by a process called "eidetic reduction," working back through previous experience of the phenomenon until one arrives at the first experience of the phenomenon, or the "primitive fact." During this process of eidetic reduction, one attempts to realize and bracket out any bias, prejudice, unconscious influences, or preconceptions that might have transformed or influenced the *meaning* of the phenomenon. Ultimately, one attains the "essence" of the reality free from distortion. From this vantage point, one

can investigate the import and effect of the "bracketed" prejudices and reintegrate them into the knowing experience.[2]

David Tracy has pointed out that the method of phenomenology has undergone many refinements since Husserl,[3] and that the analytic process of translating the symbols and gestures of everyday life and language has benefited the theologian by pointing increasingly to the religious dimension of our lives. At risk of oversimplification, we shall attempt to exemplify this approach as an aid toward a better understanding of the efficacy of sacraments.

As we said above, phenomenology is concerned with describing and understanding experiences, human actions, or events as they appear to us in their proper and total context. Assume then that reality is understood not just in terms of its material composition but also in terms of its *function*.[4] For example, a mass of concrete placed horizontally in a building is called a floor. The same concrete mass raised vertically in a building is called a wall.

Using the same approach to study and understand human activity, we are prompted to examine once more the function of symbols in human interaction. Our existence as bodies places us in a symbolic situation where we must use words and gestures to express our inner self to those around us. We use our body to express ourself and our intended meaning to others.

In turn, meaning is not something we assign arbitrarily to our actions. For example, the objects we use already have a certain objectivity to their use. A person may sign a letter-bomb "With love," or pretend to send a gift that is actually poison, but all the protestations of love and concern cannot defuse or transform the built-in destructive power of the object he is sending.

The Person Is in the Symbol

In short, there is a conjunction between *person* and *symbol*.[5] We cannot divorce the *person* that we are from the *symbols* that we use. A faithful husband, for example, bestows a kiss on his wife; knowing the type of person he is, she responds receptively and lovingly. In this case the symbol is authentic; behind the symbol of loving concern stands a truly loving husband. Person and symbol correspond authentically.

But suppose an unfaithful husband mockingly embraces his wife, pretending to be a loyal spouse. Knowing of his infidelities, the wife recoils from his hypocrisy. In this case the symbol is dishonest; the person that he truly is cannot be concealed by the gesture of pretense. In short, the gestures we use, the actions we carry out, are intrinsically bound up with who we are; by those who know us, they are recognized readily as either honest or dishonest.

Application to Sacraments

When we apply this philosophic analysis to the symbolic acts called sacraments, it may be easier for us to understand the traditional mind of the Church when she tells us that through these symbols, Christ himself is truly active. The very person of Christ reaches out to us through the symbol that is his Church and the sacramental actions that we as "Church" join in celebrating. Sacramental actualization or efficacy is thus supported by contemporary phenomenology.

Husserl's phenomenology seems to have influenced another contemporary approach to sacramental theory—namely, that of Tad Guzie in his text, *The Book of Sacramental Basics*.[6] His analysis of what he calls the rhythm of life (reflected also in the sacraments) includes three aspects: the *"lived experience"* (cf. Husserl), the *retelling of the experience* in story form, and the *festive occasion*.

"Lived experience," according to Guzie, is to be distinguished from "raw experience," such as routine actions, undifferentiated events that make no special impression upon one and do not call forth any special reflection. The "lived experience," however, is that phenomenon that one interprets as having special meaning (e.g., meeting a close friend who gives needed support at a crucial moment of my life; a moment such as marriage, the birth of my first child, some special accomplishment in my professional or business career, etc.)

My personal lived experience is, in turn, linked with and evaluated within a larger "history"—the corporate human experience of which my history may be but an infinitesimal part. I am part of many communities—family, neighborhood, nation, religious body—and each of these helps me to interpret the significance of an event in my life.

Furthermore, I am moved to share my meaningful experience with others—this is the storytelling phase of the life-rhythm. Finally, my sharing of the story with others occurs most fittingly within some festive occasion, perhaps a family reunion, some anniversary, or a holiday celebration. Thus the rhythm of life is really the process by which we *live*, *name*, and *frame* our experience.[7]

The application of this life-rhythm to the liturgical or sacramental level is not hard to surmise. The lived experience (initiation, attainment of maturity, forgiveness, healing, marriage, etc.), insofar as it is a *common* human experience, affords the basis on which Christ has created the sacraments. Furthermore, the individual's celebration of a sacrament must be viewed ultimately within the perspective of the total Christ-event, especially the paschal mystery, which is symbolically reenacted in every sacrament. This is the "larger history" within which each sacrament must be located.

The "storytelling" phase of the liturgical rhythm is verified in the liturgical recital or proclamation that explains what is being done in the sacrament. Such storytelling finds its natural expression in the moment of sacramental celebration. In the eucharist, for example, we retell the story of what Jesus did at the Last Supper in order to understand what we are doing when we celebrate eucharist. At the same time, this sacramental event becomes a lived experience for us as we enter into the larger framework of the Last Supper-death-resurrection event. Thus the original "lived experience" of Christ's saving death-resurrection is memorialized, re-presented symbolically, and its benefits for humanity are celebrated and acknowledged in the individual sacramental occurrence.

CHRIST ACTS IN THE SACRAMENTS: THE VIEW FROM HISTORY

Phenomenology seeks a fuller understanding of human reality by examining things in their proper context. Sacraments then must also be examined in the light of their history and practice in order to clarify the Church's understanding of their actualizing power.

Scripture

As noted above (Chapter 3), the New Testament provides only scant evidence for what today we call sacramental efficacy. It does attribute divine power to baptism (Acts 2:38; Jn. 3:5) and announces Jesus as one who would "baptize with the Holy Spirit" (Jn. 1:33). Paul see baptism as an actual immersion into Christ's paschal death and resurrection (Rom. 6:3ff.). In other words, the charter event that binds us to Christ is somehow present and reenacted in the sacramental ritual.

Likewise, the eucharistic institution narratives (Mk. 14, Mt. 26, 1 Cor. 11, and Lk. 22) show Jesus presiding at a ritual meal in which he asserts that the bread and wine become his "body" and "blood," sealing a new covenant between God and man. Paul interprets the eucharist as a genuine "proclamation" of the death of Jesus until he comes again (1 Cor. 11:26). There is no gainsaying the realism in Paul's mind as he links the Lord's Supper with the saving death of Jesus.

Furthermore, Jesus confers upon Peter the power of the keys and of "binding and loosing" (Mt. 16); the latter prerogative is repeated for the other eleven in Matthew 18 and John 20 (forgiveness of sins). But overall, relatively little *explicit* attestation appears in the New Testament that Christ himself would continue acting in the ritual functions of the community. One reason is simply that the principal focus of the New Testament is on the community's role of proclaiming the presence of God's Kingdom in the person of Jesus. The proclamatory and missionary role is predominant.

The Fathers

As the Christian community developed, however, clearer affirmations appear that Christ is ultimately the one who "baptizes," "forgives sins," and "feeds us" in the eucharistic sacrificial-meal. The Fathers of the Church often refer to the sacraments as actions of Christ using the ministry of men. St. John Chrysostom asserts: "Neither angel nor archangel can do anything with regard to what is given from God; but the Father, the Son, and the Holy Ghost, dispenses all, while the priest lends his time and affords his hand."[8] St. Ambrose, referring to baptism, states: "Damasus has not cleansed, Peter has not cleansed, Ambrose has not cleansed, Gregory has not cleansed; for the service is ours but the sacraments are yours [i.e., Christ's]. For it is not of human power to confer divine things, but it is your function, Lord, and that of the Father."[9] St. Augustine, commenting on the text of John 4:2 that Jesus himself did not baptize but his disciples, has this to say:

"He and not He: He by power, they by ministry; they performed the service of baptizing, the power of baptizing remained in Christ. His disciples, then, baptized and a Judas was still among his disciples; were those, then, whom Judas baptized not again baptized; and those whom John baptized, were they again baptized? Plainly there is a repetition, but not a repetition of the same baptism. For those whom John baptized, John baptized; those whom Judas baptized, *Christ baptized*. In like manner, then, they whom a drunkard baptized, those whom a murderer baptized, those whom an adulterer baptized, if it was the baptism of Christ, were baptized by Christ."[10]

Regarding the eucharist, John Chrysostom says: "Believe, therefore, that even now it is that supper at which he himself sat down. For this is in no way different from that other one; but both this and that are his own work. When therefore you see the priest delivering it unto you, reckon not that it is the priest that does this, but that it is Christ's hand that is stretched out."[11] In the same vein St. Ambrose, in his work *On the Sacraments*, asserts:

"You perhaps say: 'My bread is usual.' But that bread is bread before the words of the sacrament; when consecration has been added, from bread it becomes the flesh of Christ. So let us confirm this, how it is possible that what is bread is the body of Christ.

"By what words, then, is the consecration, by whose expressions? By those of the Lord Jesus . . . thus the expression of Christ performs this sacrament."[12]

From these random samples of some of the Fathers, it is abundantly clear that for them, it is ultimately Christ who is acting in the sacramental rituals through his ministers, the priests of the Church. Thus both Christ and the Church are involved in the sacramental event. "The Eucharist makes the Church, and the Church makes the Eucharist."[13]

In summation, then, we may say that the Fathers were convinced that divine power is operative in the sacraments. It is not uncommon, however, especially for the later Christian authors, to speak of Christ being *contained* especially in the eucharist, or that somehow we are identified with Christ in the sacramental action. Nevertheless, the conviction is general that the power of the sacraments ultimately is traceable to Christ himself.

The Scholastic Period

Causality: Contrast between East and West
For the Fathers of the East, it was sufficient to maintain that somehow Christ is the ultimate cause of the power of the sacraments. They also often refer to Christ giving them the Spirit, or acknowledge the presence of the Spirit in the sacramental act. But they show no particular concern for the *mode* of sacramental causality, that is, the way in which the sacraments produce their effect. It was the Western theologian Peter Lombard in the twelfth century who introduced a philosophic concept of *cause* to explain the realization of sacramental power. The topic of efficacy, or how the sacraments work, was much discussed, especially in terms of what is necessary for a valid or true sacrament and what is required for a lawful or fruitful reception of the sacrament. Attention to causality eventually overshadowed the revelatory and celebrational function of the sacraments. The danger then arose of overemphasizing the rite itself in a kind of magical or mechanical way.

Thomas Aquinas: Instrumental Physical Causality
Thomas Aquinas, the great synthesizer of Scholastic
theology, was not certain at the beginning of his career
as a theologian whether he should define a sacrament
in terms of sign or in terms of cause. In the *Summa
Theologica*, he makes his choice and defines the sacraments in terms of sign. When he comes to define the
efficacy of the sacraments and to explore just *how*
Christ acts in the sacraments, however, he falls back
on the concept of cause, but does so with important
qualifications. He opts for physical causality as opposed to a purely moral or juridical causality.[14] Within
the Aristotelian category of physical causality, he
chooses instrumental physical causality.[15]

For Thomas, several instruments or agents operate in
the sacraments. The Son of God, the Divine Person, is
the chief agent who works through his sacred humanity, which Thomas called a "conjoined instrument"
(so-called because the human nature of Christ was personally united to divinity in the second Person of God
himself). The son of God acting through his body
works in turn through a series of "separate" instruments: the priest of the Church and the elements and
words of the sacramental matter and form, which
mediate Christ's "grace" through the senses of the
body and ultimately to our inmost self.

We may observe here that, outside of a mention of the
minister of the Church, Thomas moves almost directly
from the action of Christ to that of the sacraments
without emphasizing the function of the Church. This
is because at that time there was not a highly developed ecclesiology; treatises on the Church were just
beginning to be written. Therefore Thomas proceeds
more directly on an individual basis from Christ to the
priest to the sacramental act.

Christ's Passion: Ultimate Source of Sacramental Power

To his credit, Aquinas did not fail to point out that the ultimate historical source of power in the sacraments was the passion of Christ.

"The sacraments of the Church, in a special way, derive their power from the passion of Christ, a power which is passed on to us in some way by the reception of the sacraments. As a sign of this 'there flowed from the side of Christ hanging on the cross water and blood,' the one referring to baptism, the other to the Eucharist, which are the most powerful of the sacraments."[16]

Like so many of the Fathers before him, Thomas interprets the effusion of blood and water from the pierced side of Christ on the cross in both a sacramental and an ecclesial sense. For it is baptism and the eucharist that are most necessary for the continuance and the vitality of the Church, baptism giving it new members and the eucharist sustaining it by Christ's sacrificial love celebrated and shared by the community. Therefore, at least implicitly, Thomas does see the Church as a necessary nexus between the paschal mystery of Jesus and the celebration and gift of the sacraments.

Two Effects of Sacraments

In the twelfth and thirteenth centuries, the Scholastic theologians spoke of three components of sacraments: (1) the *sacramentum tantum*, the external rite alone (for example, the pouring of water accompanied by the word-formula in baptism); (2) the *res et sacramentum*, a first effect of the sacrament, a spiritual *res* or reality caused by the external rite, which in turn is a symbol, or *sacramentum*, of the ultimate effect, grace (we may venture to translate the phrase *res et sacramentum* as the "symbolic reality"); and (3) the *res tantum*, the grace alone, that is, the ultimate reality conferred by the sacrament.

The *Res et Sacramentum* (Symbolic Reality): In those
sacraments that are traditionally never repeated—that
is, baptism, confirmation, and orders—the symbolic
reality came to be called the *character*, variously described as a seal or brand or mark on the soul, that in
turn was the cause of the grace that followed.[17] The
character, then, was said to dispose the recipient to
receive the grace made available by the valid conferral
of the sacrament and its effect. The second or ultimate
effect, namely grace, would actually be attained only if
the recipient was properly disposed. The latter graced
condition is known as the fruitfulness of the sacrament.

Concerning the significance of the character, the
Fathers of the Church considered it a sealing in the
name of the Trinity or, more particularly, of Christ,
since it is his imprint or image on the believer. St.
Thomas, however, added a new dimension to the
character by considering the characters of baptism,
confirmation, and orders as specifically oriented toward Christian worship. They configure or conform
the Christian to Christ the priest. They delegate the
Christian to share with Christ in his worship of the
Father.[18] Thus for St. Thomas, the character confers a
certain competence or a commission within the community of the Church, a participation in varying degrees in the priestly worship of Christ toward the
Father. This Thomistic view remains, however, a
theological opinion, since the Church has made no
dogmatic pronouncement upon the precise nature or
function of the character.

While the symbolic reality of baptism, confirmation,
and orders came to be called the character, a symbolic
reality or a first effect occurs also in other sacraments.
In the eucharist, the symbolic reality is the body and
blood of Christ present under the bread and wine
symbols. In matrimony, it is the spiritual bond created

between Christian husband and wife, a bond that lasts until the death of either party. Finally, in reconciliation and the anointing of the sick, authors acknowledge the conferral of a certain adornment or embellishment of the soul (*ornatus animae*). In reconciliation, it is said to be the creation of an interior spirit of repentance or perhaps reconciliation with the Church; in the anointing of the sick, it is a spiritual anointing that remits venial sins, or removes the "scars" of sin and prepares for entrance into glory.

In modern times (beginning in the last decades of the nineteenth century), theologians have come to stress the ecclesial dimension of the symbolic reality; that is, more and more they have come to view this first or intermediate effect of the sacraments as creating in the recipient a special relationship to the visible Church. Toward the end of the last century, Matthias Scheeben maintained that the symbolic reality unites us in a special way with Christ as head of his mystical body.[19] He likens the condition of the Christian marked by a sacramental character to the hypostatic union with Christ. Just as the humanity of Jesus of Nazareth was personally united to the Son of God and through him to the Father and the Spirit, thereby drawing upon itself the fullness of grace, so the Christian marked with the character or symbolic reality of the sacrament is united to Christ in and through his Church, and gains access to the special sacramental graces flowing from the head to the members. In support of this ecclesial dimension of the sacramental character, Schillebeeckx cites a constant tradition from the time of St. Augustine through the Middle Ages up to the present, a factor present despite differences in theological systems, a constant belief that "a person who bears a character or mark bears a certain relation to the visible ecclesial community."[20]

The *Res Tantum* (Grace): The *res et sacramentum* leads

to the final or maximal effect, the *res tantum*, that is, the *grace* produced by a given sacrament. This grace would be actualized in the recipient only if he is properly disposed (Trent: "places no obstacle in the way"). Once the number of sacraments was officially settled (Lateran IV, 1215) and repeated by Trent (1545–1563), the search was begun for special graces attached to each sacrament. It was theorized that each sacrament must have a particular purpose and, therefore, must actualize or confer the grace-power needed to fulfill the goal of that sacrament.

Baptism would confer the grace of Christian vocation to fulfill one's responsibilities as a son or daughter of God. Confirmation seals us with the Spirit to complete the commitment begun at baptism. The eucharist, at least according to Aquinas, confers the grace of unity in the mystical Body, the Church; it is, therefore, first of all a communal grace, a gift of solidarity in the fellowship of love established by Christ. The vocational sacraments of matrimony and orders confer the "grace of state"—that is, the grace to carry out the duties of those respective states of life in the ecclesial community. The sacraments of reconciliation and anointing of the sick confer Christ's healing grace according to the recipient's need—to heal the sinner by restoring him to full communion with the assembly, or to heal the ailing person in spirit by forgiveness of sins and, God willing, also to confer bodily healing and active restoration to the ecclesial assembly. Such was the rationalization for seven sacraments, each answering a particular need of the individual Christian. (Later, theologians such as Schillebeeckx would view the "seven" distinct graces of the sacraments as a sign of messianic plenitude.)

Grace Caused by Signification
Regarding the grace that is offered concurrently with the *res et sacramentum*, Aquinas argued that this grace

is caused precisely by the signifying power of the sacraments. They effect exactly what they signify and they do so precisely by signifying it.[21] In this way, he joins sign and cause most intimately. In other words, he sees a very close connection between the effect of the sacrament and its ritual celebration. The net result of this Thomistic emphasis on grace being signified and caused at the same time opens the way to an understanding that grace must be manifested or "made visible" in some way. This concept leads us to the next stage of our consideration of actualization, the Church, which is a most necessary visible agent in the trilogy of Christ, Church, and man, all of whom have a part to play in carrying out the sacramental events among us.

THE CHURCH'S ROLE IN THE ACTUALIZATION OF SACRAMENTS

Church as Sacrament or Fullness of Christ

One of the most celebrated contributions of Vatican II to contemporary ecclesiology was its return to the concept of the Church as sacrament of Christ; that is to say, the Church is an extension or prolongation of Christ and his saving grace in the present life of man. What Paul called the "fullness of Christ" (*pleroma*) is nothing other than the full communion of all those bound to Christ as his members. "Church" therefore means Head and members together. The Son of God, retaining his glorified humanity, has joined to himself a vast assembly of the faithful. As the risen Head of this body, the Son of God still acts through his humanity and through his social body, the Church, joined to his risen flesh. In this way, the Church's fundamental saving acts cannot be mere human acts. It is precisely because the Church is forever joined to its risen Head that the grace of Christ is passed on to his members, to the community that is bound to him. This is why we may call the Church, in its most comprehensive sense, a sacrament or symbol of the living Christ among us.

The Church is a living manifestation of that saving and victorious grace available to us through the paschal mystery of her Head. It is for this reason, namely that the Church is the extension or fullness of its Head, that it is able to actualize the divine reality of salvation that proceeds from the risen Jesus. The Church's acts are indeed the acts of Christ.

Church as Symbol of a World Charged with Grace
Sacraments are acts of the Church in its role as the basic sacrament of the world's salvation, realizing itself concretely in the life situation of its members. The Church symbolizes the grace that is always at work in the world. The Church is always in union with Christ; in the sacramental celebration, the Church makes concrete this union with Christ to whom it has committed itself. This is what the medieval theologians called the *opus operatum*, that is, the actual deed accomplished in the sacramental celebration.

The Church cannot "lose" Christ's grace, since it has committed itself to him especially in the sacramental moment. This is, in turn, the *opus operantis ecclesiae* ("work being done by the Church"). If the sacraments are continuations and actualizations of the symbolic function of the Church as basic sacrament, then they signify the grace that the Church signifies, the grace that is always at work in the world. This way of viewing how Christ acts in the sacraments may be called the theory of symbolic causality (or intrinsic symbolism) and is followed by Karl Rahner, Piet Fransen, and several other contemporary theologians. We will discuss this at greater length in the section on contemporary theories at the end of this chapter.

Ecclesial Power Linked to Intercessory Role of the Glorified Christ

The efficacy of the Church's action in the sacraments is further substantiated by reflecting on her association with Christ as high priest in heaven. As the Epistle to the Hebrews asserts, Christ "forever lives to make intercession for us" (Heb. 7:25). A certain infallibility attaches to the prayer of Christ; there is no question of the Father's willingness to answer the plea of his Son for us. It is from this that the infallibility of the Church's bestowal of grace is derived. The sacraments are moments in the life of the Church when she joins herself explicitly to the efficacious intercession of Christ before the Father; thus in the sacraments, she enjoys the same assurance of an infallible answer of grace as does Christ her Head.

That Christ continues his priestly work of intercession for us making present his paschal mystery, especially in the challenging moments of our life, is clearly stated in Vatican II's *Constitution on the Sacred Liturgy* (1963):

"To accomplish so great a work [namely our salvation and our worship of God], *Christ is always present in his Church*, especially in her liturgical celebrations. He is present in the sacrifice of the Mass, not only in the person of his minister, 'the same now offering through the ministry of the priests, who formerly offered himself on the cross,' but especially under the Eucharistic species. By his power he is present in the sacraments, so that when a man baptizes, it is really Christ himself who baptizes . . . .

"Christ indeed always associates the Church with himself in this great work wherein God is perfectly glorified and men are sanctified . . . .

"Rightly then the liturgy is considered as an exercise of the priestly office of Jesus Christ . . . . In the liturgy the whole public worship is performed by the mystical body of Jesus Christ, that is, by the head and his members.

"From this it follows that every liturgical celebration, because it is an action of Christ, the priest, and of his body which is the Church, is a sacred action surpassing all others; no other action of the Church can equal its efficacy by the same title and to the same degree."[22]

The Church Expresses Its Role as Agent in Christ's Name
The Church has always been conscious that she is acting in Christ's name. All we have to do is listen to the sacramental word which the Church speaks in celebrating the sacraments. In the eucharistic prayer, the Church appropriates to itself the very words of Christ at the Last Supper, "This is my body. . . . This is my blood." It is not of course the flesh and blood of the ordained priest that is meant, but the flesh and blood of Christ himself. In other words, the high priest Jesus is himself consecrating and offering the eucharistic sacrifice through his Spirit, who is summoned (*epiclesis*) both upon the elements to be consecrated and upon the celebrating community to make it one. The presiding priest thus proclaims thanksgiving for God's saving deeds in the past, and invokes his presence in the here and now of the sacramental event.

In baptism, the sacramental act is celebrated in the name of all three persons of the Blessed Trinity. In confirmation, the Church declares: "Be sealed with the gift of the Holy Spirit." In the new ritual of reconciliation, the priest prays: "Through the ministry of the Church, may God give you pardon and peace, and I absolve you from your sins in the name of the Father and of the Son, and of the Holy Spirit." In the sacrament of orders, the bishop requests God the Father Almighty through Christ and his Spirit to invest his servants with the dignity of the priesthood. In mat-

116

rimony, the priest as official witness of the Church ratifies the marital covenant in the name of the Blessed Trinity. Finally, in the anointing of the sick, the Church appeals to Christ himself to help the recipient with the grace of the Holy Spirit and grant forgiveness and healing.

The Church Acts through Its Ministers

The Church acts concretely in its liturgical functions through its ministers. The liturgical leader ministers to the sacramental action, that is to the community that celebrates in symbol its Christian faith. Instead of calling this liturgical leader an instrument of Christ in the Church, it might be better to call him a "sacrament within a sacrament." Though he does not cease to act as a member of the assembled community and to be part of the corporate symbol which that community is, the priestly minister actualizes in special fashion the presence of the risen Christ in his own priestly action. Because the assembled group of Christians know the priest to be a member of the ordained ministry, the presiding priest represents the local congregation and through it the larger Church.

Furthermore, the priest personifies the unity in faith of the assembled Christians, and his words and actions represent that corporate faith; thus the presiding liturgical leader speaks for Christ, the entire Church, the corporate liturgical ministry, and the local community in its act of worship. The priest himself is a kind of word, clarifying the experienced event of sacramental action, so that it can more effectively function to shape the community's faith.

In the very act of worship, then, the presiding liturgical minister helps bring to being a living liturgical or worshiping community. His ministry is to foster a sense of the reality of Christ's presence in the assembled congregation, to create a unifying atmosphere, and to share his own faith and hope with his Christian brothers and sisters.

Thus we may say the minister of the worship-action acts in the name of Christ, in the name of the whole Church, as well as in the name of the liturgical assembly before him. He is indeed a mediator through whom the risen Christ is able to be more explicitly present to the assembled community; at the same time, these assembled Christians are enabled to respond to Christ's self-gift by committing themselves "to be for others," for Christ and for their fellow human beings. In his word, then, Christ and the community meet and commune.

The officially delegated minister of the Church is not always a member of the ministerial or ordained priesthood. In the case of matrimony, for example, the principal ministers of the sacrament are the bride and groom themselves who, in the presence of the priest as official witness of the ministerial Church and the community, solemnly covenant themselves to each other for life in the sacramental state of matrimony. Likewise, in the case of emergency baptism, a lay person, even a nonbeliever, may celebrate this sacrament validly so long as he performs the sacrament the way the Church performs it and has the intention of doing what the Church does, which is always required of every ecclesial minister.

We live in a time of expanding Church ministries, in which the baptized faithful participate more actively in the ongoing mission of the Church. We have permanent deacons, lay ministers of the eucharist, lectors, acolytes, ministers of music, and ministers of hospitality (ushers) who contribute actively to sacramental *worship*. But if we use the word "sacramentality" in an extended sense, we may claim in a way that all the Church's service activities are "sacramental": symbols of Christ acting upon the world. All of the various ministries now developing—religious education, service to the sick and the poor, the promotion of peace and justice, the many specialized ministries to various groups such as youth, divorced and remarried persons, the mentally retarded, the aged, the alcoholic, in short the practice of the traditional spiritual and corporal works of charity—all in a wider sense could be classified as actualizing the Church's, and therefore Christ's, presence to humankind.

THE COMMUNITY'S AND THE INDIVIDUAL'S ROLE IN THE ACTUALIZATION OF GRACE

Dialogical Context

We cannot consider the presence of Christ's saving deeds among us without also considering the necessary response on the part of the participants in these sacramental actions. Truly it is one thing for Christ through his Church to reach out to us in the power of his paschal mystery; it is another thing to consider both the community's and the individual's acceptance of this offer of Christ. Just as in the case of God's word demanding faith-acceptance, so here we may use the analogy of the covenant, which is both invitation and response. God calls to us through the sacraments of his Church and likewise awaits humanity's response to his call of love and healing. In a sense, the efficacy of the sacrament depends both on the quality of the proclamation made through the Church, thanks to symbol and word, and on its reception by the individual and the entire community.

Witness and Proclamation

The actualization of the power of the sacraments is not completed until there is an actual transformation on the part of all to whom the Church's action and Christ's action are directed. The Church indeed has the vocation of being a sacrament, not only by conferring

119

or making available the saving and healing grace of Christ, but also by being a witness to and proclaiming the word of God. An example may be given in the case of the anointing of the sick.[23] Let us suppose a person in the prime of life has been attacked suddenly by serious illness. He learns that he has contracted cancer; he has only a few months to live. When he learns of the inevitability of death, he is filled at first with anger and despair. But gradually the Church enters the picture, not as an abstraction but through persons who embody it. His wife, a priest, a friend, or a relative helps him to see his disease along with his entire life in the light of hope. The proclamation of the message of hope penetrates his spirit. Slowly the sick man regains hope and the Christian outlook on his disease and his life. Instead of giving way to despair, he finds a way that opens into the future. Gradually he becomes more and more serene, until he ends by accepting his death in the Christian perspective of the ultimate future and the total fulfillment promised him at his baptism.

Once this process has taken place, thanks to the sacramental action of the Church made visible in human beings, this Christian, together with Christ and the Church, can now celebrate his pilgrimage of faith at a critical moment in his life. In this instance, we have what can be called the sacramental grace of the anointing of the sick, where anointing includes not just the rite itself but the entire pastoral approach to the sacrament. Is it not a grace that this person should find the presence of Christ in this particular moment of his life, not only in the sacraments but also in the presence of those who have helped him respond in faith to the proffered healing of Christ, which only now can be effectively operative in him? Thus in this case, the actualization of the sacrament of the anointing of the sick includes the transformation of the individual, a transformation resulting from the action of Christ, the Church, and the recipient himself, who has responded to the invitation of Christ as symbolized or sacramentalized by the Christian community.

The Ambience of Sacramental Transformation
When analyzing the place of human beings in the actualization of the sacraments, we should not think that it is only the individual recipient who benefits from the sacrament. If we wish to restore the community to its true position in sacramental theology, that is, making a sacrament in some sense the celebration of the whole community, we must allow for the grace-effects to touch all of those involved in the sacramental celebration. For example, when parents on the occasion of their child's baptism genuinely rediscover the meaning of their own baptism, they too are sharing in the grace of the sacrament. In this way, as the Church reexpresses its own mystery of faith on the occasion of some specific state in the lives of people, it effects its own transformation. Its message more fully penetrates and transforms even those who proclaim it.

Thus it may be said that, ultimately, sacramental efficacy enables one to discover not only who God and Christ are, but also one's own self, what one is now, and what one is called to become. It can exercise a humanizing influence upon a person as well as a divinizing one. It helps a person to be truly human, encouraging fulfillment of one's true human potential, and to realize those so-called natural virtues or basically good and sound inclinations that are present in a person's particular nature. Insofar as one is prompted to fulfill one's own human dignity, a person is more ready to be transformed and to transform himself or herself in accordance with the vision of God and with the eschatological image of humanity as revealed in Jesus.

Rahner's Theory

Sacraments are sometimes considered as special moments in an otherwise profane existence. In other words, daily life is thought to be relatively unholy, secular, and profane; the purpose of the sacraments is to gain strength and grace for continuing to lead our existence in a drab, dull, routine world apart from God. Karl Rahner, among others, challenges this view of reality by asking: Are the sacraments really peak experiences? Does the average person experience a sacramental moment as a decision-making moment, a moment of special commitment to Christ, a decisive moment in his life? Is there not a danger of a kind of empty ritualism? So often does there seem to be any real difference between the moment of the sacraments and the moment of our daily life? Do the sacraments really improve our daily commitment to Christ? Do they merely give us the power to "be good"? Are they among the "good works" which all Christians are called to perform?

In keeping with the current mode of doing theology by reading the signs of the times, we are prompted to reevaluate the authenticity of every practice and experience, including the reception of the sacraments. If we call sacraments peak moments or privileged moments, we ought to realize that the *kairos*, or basic decision-making moment, is actually quite infrequent. According to Rahner, sacraments are actually part of a larger cosmic history of grace. The whole world is charged with God's saving power, his loving outreach, his presence to humankind. Sacraments are signs or manifestations in one's own life of the grace that guides the history of the whole world. This grace is omnipresent, but of course one may cut himself off from the saving God by a culpable "no."

Rahner maintains that the world is permanently graced at its root, the inmost center of conscious subjects. There is a radical gracing of reality. Therefore, grace is not a particular phenomenon parallel to the rest of human life but the ultimate depth of everything the spiritual creature does when he realizes himself. When he laughs, cries, loves, lives and dies, hopes against hope, reaches out with care and concern for others, in all these moments he is led to the infinity and victory that is God. Grace, therefore, is the holiness of all that is profane.[24]

Grace creates a solidarity among mankind; we all experience the same human destiny, and Christ is the clearest manifestation of this grace at the heart of ordinary living. Therefore, there is a liturgy of the world. Sharing in the Mass and the other sacraments celebrates what is really happening in the world; it leads to the divine depths of real life. Worship ritualizes the experience of grace in everyday life, in so-called "profane" life. The Mass, therefore, is a kind of tiny sign of the "Mass" of the world.

In justification of this, Rahner cites that in the Scriptures (Acts 10), the Roman officer, Cornelius, already received the Holy Spirit before his baptism by Peter. He also cites the example of a penitent receiving the virtue of charity to make an act of love even before he approaches sacramental penance or reconciliation. This leads him to ask: How then can the sacraments be explained in their activity as privileged moments of grace? May not grace be present to us in the whole world in which we live, and the sacraments be explained as culminating points or capsulating moments of the grace that is already in the world redeemed by Christ?

The sacraments, then, for Rahner and the school of symbolic causality are acts of the Church, which is the

basic sacrament of the world's salvation, realizing itself concretely in the life situation of an individual.
The Church symbolizes the grace that is always at
work in the world. The Church, by virtue of the fact
that it is joined to its Head, makes present more tangi-
bly the saving grace of Christ with which the world
has already been charged. Through its faith-
commitment (fidelity) to Christ with special constancy,
the Church as his body verifies and bears witness to
the existence of grace in daily life. In this view, then,
the sacraments have no monopoly on Christ gracing
men; they are rather privileged events that concretize
the grace that is already at work in the world around
us. They are signals that God is present to his world,
embracing it and drawing it to himself. (cf. Jn. 3:16,
12:32). Therefore, Christians, like the ministerial
Church and the sacraments, are to be witnesses to
others that God is embracing them too. In this kind of
"evangelization," Christians themselves are graced by
their witness of God's power acting upon them; others
outside the Church, profiting from this witness, are
themselves attracted to the Church, the basic sacrament, and thereby acquire a certain "relationship"
(e.g., desire) to it.

According to Rahner, such a view does not diminish
the power or efficacy of sacraments nor minimize or
diminish their value. It simply serves to locate them
more authentically in the history of human experience.
The human person's awareness of this experience, together with his self-consciousness, helps him to explain the phenomenon of his relationship to God and
grace and the world of salvation. This is, in effect, a
kind of correlation theology that approaches modern
problems in the light of both the divine message and
the data of the contemporary life-context. It
exemplifies the shift in consciousness that we spoke of
in the introduction to this book. We cannot do theol-

ogy in a vacuum; we must be aware of what is happening around us and somehow explain these phenomena in terms of God's perennial message as it comes down to us through Scripture and tradition, as well as through the verification of human experience today.

Kiesling's "Paradigm" Approach
A further development of Rahner's theory of symbolic causality and of his conviction that the whole world is charged with grace is found in the theology of Christopher Kiesling.[25] According to Kiesling, all created agents and their activities are phenomena of grace, natural symbols of God's self-giving and transforming action. The whole world around us is sacramental, that is, charged with divine grace. We in turn must articulate our experience of this grace around us and interpret it by institutionalized or patterned action. This may be done on a natural level, as for example in the relationship between man and woman, the lifestyle that husband and wife live in love for each other, a lifestyle of commitment and fidelity. Or it may take the form of a more planned and "ritualized" activity, such as the way in which a nation celebrates its origins by flying flags, having parades, shooting off fireworks, having speeches, and so on, as we do on July Fourth.

Kiesling goes on to ask: What is unique then about the seven sacraments, beyond the sacramentality of the world? He answers by suggesting that there are four qualities that serve to set apart Christian sacraments as central models ("paradigms") of the grace activity that goes on around us in our daily experience. The *first* characteristic of sacrament as paradigm of grace is that it is a more *explicit* phenomenon of God's graciousness towards us, expressed in a ritual action that has special consequences for us. *Second*, it is a more *personalized* grace. We realize this, for example, when in the liturgy of baptism the priest says "John (or Mary), I baptize you in the name of the Father, etc." The sacrament is directed specifically and articulately to an individual. *Third*, the sacramental paradigm is a climactic moment of God's self-donation to an *individual* and the individual's response. It takes place especially at the juncture or boundary moments of his life, such as birth, maturity, marriage, death. *Fourth*, a sacramental paradigm is *public*; that is, it is recognized by the community as central to its corporate life. The whole community of the Church is involved, for example, in the initiation of new members; the introduction of members into adulthood, as in confirmation; the establishment of a new family unit, as in matrimony; the ordination of priests and bishops, and so on.

In applying this to the individual sacrament, Kiesling goes on to suggest that in terms of the framework of our daily experience, each individual sacrament functions as a paradigm or model of the grace we experience in other happenings of our life. For example, baptism is a paradigm of entrance into various human communities, such as that of family, city, nation, labor union, political party, school, and so on. Confirmation is a paradigm of commitment to some worthy cause, to certain ideals, to various human associations such as those promoting justice, peace, and so on. Penance or reconciliation is a paradigm or model of all forms of human reconciliation, whether between members of families or of other communities, between proponents of opposing ideas of government, or even between rival nations. Anointing of the sick is paradigmatic of the sacramentality of all care of the bodily and mentally ill, the economically and culturally deprived, the oppressed and the rejected. Ordination is paradigmatic of the sacramentality of all human responsibility for the welfare of others, especially their common welfare, of all human leadership and government, whether in the restricted circle of the family or the wider circle of international life. The eucharist is paradigmatic of the sacramentality of all self-sacrifice for others, and for the causes of justice, love, freedom, and truth. It is paradigmatic of the sacramentality of every meal that people share and of all human sharing, whether economic, cultural, or spiritual. Marriage is paradigmatic of the sacramentality of every human encounter, every human friendship, all human love. It is paradigmatic also of the more ordinary experiences of daily social life of every kind. The word of God, Scripture and the oral tradition preceding it, as well as the words of God's spokesmen underlying them, may also be added to this list as paradigmatic of the sacramentality of all human speech and communication.

According to Kiesling, then, the seven sacraments as given us by Christ, the apostles, and the Church more than satisfy the basic needs of human existence. If there is any deficiency, it is not in the number of the sacraments, but in the way in which they are celebrated. The great need of our time, according to Kiesling, is in recognizing that the sacraments are pointers to or signals of the grace that is all about us and needs to be exploited and reaped. Every moment of new birth, reconciliation, joy, and love is a moment of trysting with the Father, the Son and the Holy Spirit. Grace is everywhere, and the sacraments serve to remind us of that fact and in turn to commission us to recognize the existence of the divine in the human environment in which we live. The sacred and the profane are not disparate experiences of reality, but rather they coalesce, producing a unity in the experience of human existence.

NOTES

1. Cf. Vatican II, *Constitution on the Church in the Modern World*, esp. articles 40 and 41.

2. George S. Worgul, Jr., *From Magic to Metaphor* (New York: Paulist Press, 1980), p. 28. Cf. David Tracy, *Blessed Rage for Order* (New York: Seabury Press, 1975), esp. pp. 47f.

3. Tracy, ibid.

4. John Macquarrie, *An Existentialist Theology* (New York: Harper & Row, 1965), pp. 54ff., where he describes Heidegger's approach to "understanding" in terms of an existential phenomenology. Things are understood in terms of their use. "What is it for?" is often the first question a child asks when confronting any novel object. "When a child lifts a spoon to his mouth, he has understood the spoon in the sense that he has discovered its instrumental character" (Ibid., p. 60).

5. Cf. Joseph M. Powers, S.J., *Eucharistic Theology* (New York: Herder & Herder, 1967), pp. 85–86.

6. Tad Guzie, *The Book of Sacramental Basics* (New York: Paulist Press, 1981).

7. Ibid., p. 23.

8. *Homilies on St. John*, 86:4.

9. *On the Holy Spirit*, Prologue, 18.

10. *On the Gospel of St. John*, Tr. 5:18.

11. *Homil. 50 in Matt.*, 3 (PG) 58, 507.

12. *On the Sacraments*, IV, Chap. 4, par. 14.

13. Cf. "The Use of the Fathers in the Constitution on the Liturgy" (original article in Italian) by Achille M. Triacca, S.D.B., in *Notitiae* 16: 168–70 (1980) 396. The expression reflects the well-known thought of St. Augustine on the close linkage between Christ's action in the *Church* and in the *sacraments*.

14. *Physical* causality views the sacramental rite itself as "containing" grace, or at least effecting a real disposition to grace (symbolic reality), in view of which God freely and really offers himself to the recipient. In *moral* causality, sacraments are less causes and more propitiatory acts or prayers that have the "moral" or persuasive effect of moving God to bestow grace. In *juridical* causality, the recipient receives a *right* or

title to grace, within a kind of contractual arrangement between himself and God. Cf. Bernard Leeming, *Principles of Sacramental Theology*, 2nd ed. (London: Longmans, 1960), pp. 287–89.

15. S.T. III, 64, 1, 3.

16. S.T. III, 62, 5.

17. St. Augustine, opposing the Donatist heretics, had maintained that their baptism was valid because it caused a certain permanent spiritual effect in the soul. Earlier, a similar decision had been reached by the Church against Cyprian of Carthage, who demanded a rebaptism of the Novatians when they rejoined the Church. The permanence of the sacrament (baptism) came to be attributed to the lasting effect ("character" or "sphragis") that the sacrament "imprints" on the soul. This theology served as a basis for the later medieval development of the *res et sacramentum*.

18. S.T. III, 63, 3.

19. Paul Palmer, S.J., "The Theology of the *res et sacramentum*," in C. Stephen Sullivan (F.S.C.) (ed.), *Readings in Sacramental Theology* (Englewood Cliffs, N.J.: Prentice-Hall, 1965), pp. 111–12. Cf. Matthias Scheeben, *The Mysteries of Christianity* (St. Louis: B. Herder, 1947), trans. Cyril Vollert (S.J.), p. 575.

20. Edward Schillebeeckx, *Christ, the Sacrament of the Encounter with God* (New York: Sheed & Ward, 1963), p. 158.

21. Cf. above, our remarks on the constitutive power of symbol (Chap. 1, pp. 15–17).

22. C.S.L., para. 7.

23. Cf. Raymond Vaillancourt, *Toward a Renewal of Sacramental Theology*, trans. Matthew J. O'Connell (Collegeville, Minn.: The Liturgical Press, 1979), p. 101.

24. Karl Rahner, S.J., "How to receive a sacrament and mean it," *Theology Digest* 19:3 (1971) 229.

25. Christopher Kiesling, O.P., "Paradigms of Sacramentality," *Worship* 44 (1970) 422–32.

Chapter Six

Models of Sacraments: Toward a Celebrational Model

In discussing the functions of sacraments, we have considered them as word-events or proclamation, and as actualizing or realizing experiences that cause Christ's paschal mystery to affect the celebrating individual and community. The third function, that of *celebration*, has been proposed as a new model for understanding "sacrament." In this chapter, we shall first consider what "model" means, what function it serves, alternate models for studying sacraments (later Scholastic, mystery-presence, and encounter) and finally, the projected celebrational model.

CONCEPT OF MODEL
What Avery Dulles has done for ecclesiology in his study, *Models of the Church*, needs to be done also for the study of sacraments.[1] Dulles studied the Church from various viewpoints: as institution, sacrament, body of Christ, people of God, herald, servant—all of these contribute something to the understanding of the Church, its nature, functions, and history. All of these approaches are necessary since no single one yields all the information needed about such a complex reality. The same must be said for sacraments.

A more technical way of labeling the above viewpoints or approaches to a subject under study is to call them models. The concept of *model*—used first by the physical, social, and behavioral sciences, and appropriated later by philosophers and theologians—has been defined by Bernard Lonergan as "an intelligible, interlocking set of terms and relations" that may be useful in attempting to describe reality or form an hypothesis.[2] Dulles recognizes two types of models in terms of their functions: *explanatory* models and *exploratory* models.[3] The former serve to synthesize what we already know or are inclined to believe about a subject. The latter are those models that lead hopefully to new insights on the subject under investigation.

The explanatory model in theology is accepted if it accounts for much biblical and traditional data, and with what history and experience tell us about Christian life. The "mustard seed" parable, for example, serves well to explain the growth of the Church through the centuries; it makes intelligible the phenomena encountered in the Christian community since its origins, its capacity for rapid expansion. Similarly, the model or parable of the "wheat and the weeds" accounts for the growth of the Church in spite of opposition encountered from within and from without, the presence of evil even in the midst of the community of grace, and so forth.

In the case of the exploratory model in theology, we do not have positive empirical verification, especially since we are working in the area of the supernatural as we seek new insights on a quite tentative basis. Empirical tests are inadequate because visible results and statistics can never by themselves tell us whether a given insight is right or wrong. Let us suggest that theological verification depends upon a kind of "corporate discernment of spirits." This is closely connected to a sort of connaturality in the realm of faith—a sense of Christ and of the interior presence of the Holy Spirit, an instinctual judgment for the things of God. For example, when anger, discord, and disgust result, this is obviously not the work of the Spirit; for

St. Paul, the fruits of the Spirit (Gal. 5:23–25) are love, joy, peace, patience, kindness, and so on.

Before suggesting a new sacramental model of *celebration*, we will first examine three alternate models that have been operative in sacramental theology during the last century. These are the models of late Scholasticism, mystery-presence, and interpersonal encounter. Examining these models will provide an historical background for measuring the uniqueness of the celebration model, which is increasingly proposed as a suitable contemporary model for understanding the sacraments.[4]

THE MODEL OF POST-FIFTEENTH-CENTURY SCHOLASTICISM

Two topics give some insight into the sacramental model of late Scholasticism: the questions of the *composition* of the sacraments and sacramental *causality*.

Development of the Thesis of Sacramental Composition
Originally the Fathers of the Church, especially Augustine, arrived at their notion of sacrament by referring to Scripture, where a ritual action is always joined to a word or prayer. Augustine viewed the sacramental rituals as consisting of matter and spirit, that is, the observed phenomena (the element) and the words pronounced while using the element. Augustine wrote: "When the word is added to the element we have a sacrament."

In the early Middle Ages, some changes occurred in Augustine's terminology. The word "element" was replaced by the word "matter," and the term "word" was replaced by the word "form." Thus "matter" and "form" entered the vocabulary of medieval sacramental theology. According to Schillebeeckx, the early Scholastics, and even Thomas Aquinas, were using these words not strictly in terms of Aristotle's analysis of matter, but rather analogically to express the earlier tradition in their contemporary Latin usage.[5] After Aquinas, however, Aristotle's idea of matter and form (hylemorphism) dominated Scholastic theology, and matter and form took on the technical meanings they had in Aristotelianism.

According to Aristotle's hylemorphic theory, every corporeal being consists essentially of matter (*materia*), a principle of indetermination, the general substratum of all corporeal things, and form (*forma*), a principle of completion and determination. The essential form and matter together comprise the substance of every corporeal being. As applied to sacraments, the materials used and the actions performed (e.g., pouring water in baptism, the bread and wine of the eucharist) were called the "matter" of the sacrament, and the word-formula accompanying the gesture or pronounced over the "matter" and determining its ultimate meaning was called the "form" of the sacrament.

As matter and form came to be separated in the sixteenth century from the earlier scriptural and patristic tradition, we begin to find a "thing-like" conception of grace. According to this later formula, matter and form together yield the *res* of the sacrament, which is grace. A sacrament came to be thought of as some *thing* that causes grace, which in turn is a *thing*. Here we see the beginnings of a kind of physical-quantitative model for sacraments. In other words, grace is something that fills the soul, almost as water fills a glass. Increase of grace likewise takes on a quantitative dimension.

The Notion of Causality
At this same time, the Scholastic authors had turned their attention to stressing the efficacy or power built into the sacramental rituals. Their intention was good enough: namely, to insure God's freedom in giving his

gifts and counteracting a too thing-like understanding of grace. However, their efforts proved unsuccessful. As we have already mentioned in an earlier chapter, the sacraments were presented as operating *ex opere operato*; that is, if the sacramental ritual is done properly according to the required matter and form and by the proper minister having the right intention, the ritual itself has a built-in power to achieve what it signifies. By the time such theories reached the popular level, however, it was easy to interpret the efficacy of the sacraments in a too mechanical or mechanistic fashion, almost like a grace machine, a vending machine that provides a certain product with only a minimum of effort on the part of the recipient.

To their credit, the great Scholastics such as Thomas Aquinas, Scotus, and Bonaventure would have abhorred such a mechanistic, almost magical approach; their successors or imitators overstressed the "automated" process of sacramental action. Little wonder then that the Protestant Reformers considered such an interpretation of sacramental operation as a manipulation of the Divine; in other words, the ritual is forcing God to do something at our command.

The earlier notion of the symbolic character of sacrament had been nearly forgotten. Validity of performance and accumulation of grace slowly became the exclusive concern of sacramental investigation and scholarship.

Limitations of the Mechanical-Physical Model
In assessing this late Scholastic model, we must note that first, grace and sacraments are not things. Grace is God freely offering himself to us. Sacraments are first and foremost symbolic activities, not a relationship between physical objects. Second, the late Scholastics failed to join the study of sacraments with the study of Christ and the Church. In other words, there was a

failure to integrate sacramentology with christology and ecclesiology. Third, this model tended to encourage a passive attitude in the recipients of the sacraments. Sacraments became a ritual that individuals attend or watch or receive, rather than community celebrations engaging their active participation. Contemporary teaching, grounded in the earliest traditions of the Church, assures us that sacraments are never merely individual affairs, but always communal symbolic activities actively engaging the whole community.

Benefits of the Late Scholastic Model of Sacraments
Later Scholastics evolved various theological schools of thought on the exact nature of sacramental efficacy. The school of *moral causality* construed the sacraments more as prayers that tried to persuade or convince God to administer grace because of the sacramental ritual. According to this view, sacraments are propitiatory acts rather than actual causes of grace. Therefore, a certain benefit followed from this view of sacraments, insofar as they were regarded as prayers or acts of worship.

A second theory, *occasional causality*, stressed that it was not the sacramental ritual itself that gave grace; that act was merely an occasion for God to bestow grace out of his total freedom. Again, this theory had a positive value in safeguarding God's gratuitous action.

Finally, the theory of *physical causality*, at least in one of its forms, considered the sacraments as instruments in the hands of God. Here, the real nature of God's activity is stressed; sacraments and grace are not imaginary. Yet because of the deficiencies already discussed, the physical-mechanical model of late Scholasticism encouraged present-day theologians to seek a new model that better accorded with human experience and the current understanding of human reality.

Historical Perspective

Our present century, especially between 1920 and 1950, witnessed a disillusionment with the earlier individualistic, mechanistic, and quantitative models for sacraments.

Many theological scholars were inspired to return to the sources of Scripture and tradition to gain fresh insights, particularly in the study of liturgy. The movement to renew Christian worship became one of the great grassroots crusades of this century. Pius X entrusted the burden of research particularly to the Benedictine communities of Solesmes in France, Maredsous and Mont-Cesar in Belgium, and Beuron and Maria Laach in Germany. One of the most notable scholars in these early stages of liturgical renewal was the distinguished Benedictine, Odo Casel (1886–1948), a monk from the abbey of Maria Laach. He eventually developed the mystery-presence model for sacraments that we will now consider.

Genesis and Content of the Mystery-Presence Model

Casel's lifelong ambition was to explore the theological aspects of the liturgy to discover the essence or core of Christian worship. Through the study of the Scriptures and the Fathers, he hoped to overcome the individualism of the late Scholastic period. At the same time, he became interested in the Greek mystery religions, which, it seemed to him, bore many resemblances to the sacraments.

The ancient Greeks felt a keen sense of fate. The "gods" controlled human destiny. The only possible escape from the fates was to join a Greek mystery religion dedicated to a certain god by initiation into its secret rituals. Through the ritual action, the initiate gained secret knowledge necessary for salvation, and at the same time relived in a ritual way the principal experiences of that god. The gods were considered to have appeared visibly on earth, undergone human suffering, and rediscovered good fortune, salvation, or eternal life. The actions and experiences of the gods were made present in sacred actions, words, and symbols. Through these rituals, the participant achieved communion with the gods, and thus attained salvation.

Casel defined the concept of *mystery* as "a sacred ritual action in which a saving deed is made present through the rite; the congregation, by performing the rite, take part in the saving act, and thereby win salvation."[6]

For Casel, there were many similarities between the Greek mystery religions and the teaching of the Greek Fathers, especially in the mystagogical catecheses, and also in St. Paul himself (passages such as Rom. 6:3; Col. 1:20, 26, 27; Eph. 1:9–10; 3:9–11). Paul speaks of the mystery as God's plan for the redemption of all mankind, hidden in God's mind from all eternity and revealed through Christ, especially through his incarnation, death, and resurrection. Casel maintained that all of these acts of Christ together constitute a single mystery, a single saving act identified as the paschal mystery, the passage of the Son of God into this world and back to the Father through death and resurrection.

For Casel, to accomplish our reunion with the Father, we too must enter into the paschal mystery of Christ's return to the eternal Kingdom. We are able to do this, to make contact with the saving deeds of Christ in history, through a new level of the mystery, that is, through the liturgy of the church. Here Casel made perhaps his most enduring contribution to twentieth-century theological development. The liturgical reform was in great measure spurred by Casel's theology of the mystery-presence. For him, the whole mystery of Christ, the whole saving life work of Jesus on earth, is somehow contained in and re-presented in the

137

Church's official worship. Over and over again in his writings, the monk of Maria Laach repeats his convictions on the mystery-presence. "The mystery is no mere recalling of Christ and His saving deed; it is a memorial in worship. The church does what the Lord did, and thereby makes His act present. Christ Himself is present and acts through the church, His *ecclesia*, while she acts with him. Both carry out the actions."[7] Again he asserts "What is past in history, the death of Christ for example, and what is in the future of history, his *parousia*, are present in the mystery."[8]

Applying his mystery-presence theory to the eucharist, he asserts:

"It is this, the making present of the sacrificial death of Christ, which Scripture and all the ancient fathers and liturgists hold to be the meaning of the Mass . . . the Lord must appear in the Mass as sacrificed and not as glorified, although in heaven he is such. . . . He brings his sacrificial death before us over and over in the Mass, in a *sacramental* manner."[9]

According to Casel, the sacramental act of worship does not merely convey to us the grace-effect of Christ's historical saving deeds, but actually and objectively renders them present, not of course in all the specific circumstances of persons and details, but as he says, in what was essential in that action, its substance. Therefore, sacraments are able to overcome all barriers of time and space. As he notes, "The whole design of salvation from the incarnation to the parousia, which has not yet appeared in point of time, does take on a sacramental presence and therefore can be the subject of our co-participation in a most vivid way."[10]

In a sense, Casel anticipates the contemporary theology of encounter, as he says:

"It is in the liturgy of the church that Christ presents his saving work to us once again. The work is fulfilled in a fully objective manner, even without us. It is the very saving work which the Father accomplished, offering the Son in His great love, bringing His Son back to Him. This saving action is what is made present to us in the mystery of worship. Because it is made present, we can be joined to Christ in all reality, we can do along with him what he does. The condition is that we give ourselves to him, as we renounce ourselves; this is the way into the action of Christ."[11]

Assessment of the Mystery-Presence Model

Positive Aspects
First, this model successfully overcomes the individualistic and mechanistic features of the late Scholastic model and returns to the rich tradition of the Church Fathers, with their emphasis on worship as communal and Christ-centered. Second, mystery-presence assures the freedom of God's self-gift to us and joins this self-gift to the historical offer of salvation made in Christ as the revelation and presence of God in the world. Grace is properly understood as a sharing in the saving acts disclosed in the person of Christ, who is really and objectively present among the worshiping community of believers. Third, mystery-presence also gives due weight to personalism. In a sense, Casel paved the way for the interpersonal encounter model developed in the late 1950s and early 1960s. Sacraments are human symbolic activities that focus on the person of Christ, the revelation of the Father. Fourth, the mystery-presence model acknowledges God as the ultimate cause of the sacramental celebration. Too often, sacraments are envisioned as creating something new. This theory reminds us that the sacraments celebrate realities that have already become present, though they are still

shrouded in mystery. Humanity will never exhaust the
activities of a God who transcends the limits of human
analysis. Sacraments do not conjure up God; they vividly make present, express, and intensify God's love
within the sacramental participants, a love that is already and always present for God's people. Fifth, we
may note the influence of Casel on many scholars after
him. As the French theologian J.H. Nicolas wrote:

"In sacramental theology, the *mysterium* theory of Dom
Casel has played the role of an active agent of fermen-
tation. . . . That the liturgy in general and the sacraments in particular are essentially a reactualization of
the acts by which our salvation is accomplished, that
the efficacy of the sacraments consists in making man
have a share—spiritually and even bodily—in these
mysteries, . . . no one today will any longer contest."[12]

Objections to the Model

First, the data available for verification and substantia-
tion of Casel's interpretation of the Greek mystery religions are meager. As secret cults, it is not surprising
that they would leave behind little documentation of
their rituals and doctrines. It is therefore difficult, if
not impossible, to determine exactly what their core or
substance actually was, and how this was related to
their overall religious synthesis. Second, perhaps Casel
was somewhat presumptuous in his assumption that
the Greek Fathers were influenced by the Greek mystery religions in their catechesis of the catechumens. In
fact, very little is known about the interpretation of the
Greek mystery religions from the texts of the Fathers.

Third, the most serious objection on philosophic
grounds is the one most often posed; namely, although
Casel insists on the presence of God and the saving
acts of Christ in the sacramental celebrations, he fails
to explain *how* this mystery-presence comes about.
There seems to be a hint that he attempted to explain

the problem through the divine-human nature of Christ's activity, that is, as a human being, Christ belongs to the order of human existence and his actions therefore are temporal and passing. As God, however, Christ's actions transcend time and have an eternal dimension.

Fourth, perhaps Casel too uncritically accepted the similarity between the pagan mystery rites and Christianity. In this, he may have been influenced by the very men whose theories he opposed, the Modernist writers of the nineteenth and early twentieth centuries, who read into the pagan mysteries more than was warranted and came to describe them in Christian language. This naturally made the resemblance between them and the Christian liturgy seem very plausible. Fifth, there has been criticism of Casel's use of the teachings of St. Paul to support his theory. Romans 6:3ff. speaks indeed of a baptismal dying and rising with Christ; 1 Cor. 11:26 affirms the eucharistic proclamation of Christ's death. Scripture authorities, however, question that Paul had anything like a mystery-presence in mind. Among the reasons assigned are these. First, Paul was probably not influenced at all by the Greek mystery cults; his thought is better explained in terms of his Judaic background. Second, besides the image of a dying and rising with Christ, Paul employs several other analogies to develop his baptismal doctrine; therefore, one is justified in looking beyond the mystery-presence concept to explain Paul's thought, perhaps in terms of corporate personality. The sacraments unite us to Christ who, as our representative, accepted the cross and the resurrection and now sacramentally allows us to share in his historical saving deed. Finally, Paul is not a theologian who thinks in terms of liturgy and mysteries, but rather primarily a preacher of the gospel belonging more to the eschatological type.[13]

Conclusively, as we have already noted, Casel's greatest contribution to the development of liturgical and theological insights probably lay in the inspiration that his mystery-presence model gave future liturgiologists.

THE INTERPERSONAL-ENCOUNTER MODEL

Sociocultural Context

Against the background of wars and social upheavals that prevailed in the latter half of the nineteenth and twentieth centuries, philosophers began to reconsider the value of the human person. Existentialism, commonly traced in its contemporary form to Soren Kierkegaard, focuses on individual human existence, and on what a person can make of himself and his life in the context in which he finds himself. Man is "being-in-the-world" (Heidegger), not just spatially, but in the sense of being bound up with, concerned for, and affected by his world.

Herewith may be discovered the two basic characteristics of an existential approach to philosophy or theology: (1) the *Fragestellung* ("manner of putting the question"), and (2) the *Begrifflichkeit*, the system of categories or concepts under which we understand what confronts us in experience, particularly as being-in-the-world.[14] For the existential theologian (e.g., Bultmann), the *Fragestellung* would involve starting with my existence as an individual and asking, "What does God or Church or sacraments mean to me?" Human existence is central to all theological problems; the Scriptures are viewed as statements primarily about man's existence. Paul's conversion story, for instance, is interpreted as his entering into a new understanding of himself. Authentic existence in the light of Scripture, then, could be described as "the perpetual appropriation of grace [as in worship], the steady orientation of the self towards the possibilities of the

142

cross and resurrection in virtue of which the believer lives not of himself but in the power of God. . . ."[15] Inauthentic existence, in contrast, is founded on worldly concern alone.

The theologian's *Begrifflichkeit* will be that "system of basic concepts derived from the philosophy of existence, which claims to have analyzed in suitable concepts the understanding of existence which is given with existence."[16] It will seek to show how human existence differs from that of mere objects in nature that lend themselves to generalization and classification.

Implicit in the focus of existential thought is concern for the value of the individual as person ("personalism") and the attainment, through free choice, of authentic personhood. While Bultmann and Heidegger tended perhaps too severely to individualism, a correction to this imbalance came to the fore in the writings of Gabriel Marcel, Martin Buber, and others who began to affirm that all human existence is fundamentally *coexistence*: it is *relational*. The individual realizes his full potentiality only by interaction with others. We may take Martin Buber in his classic work *I and Thou* as an example of this philosophic position.[16a] An "I-thou" relationship means that each affirms the other's unique value as a human being and also affirms a bond among all who share existence as humans. In communion with the other, I can perceive an experience of greater depth to life itself. Individual meaning is discovered in and flows from co-relational and co-existential life. Yet, the individual loses nothing of himself or his individuality in experiencing true community; rather, his own selfhood is developed and advanced.

Impact on Theology
From the 1940s onward, a theological reconstruction was undertaken that attempted to interpret and ex-

press Christian revelation in terms of existentialist and co-relational thought patterns. The model of "interpersonal encounter" was to be a dominant one, not only in the theology of the sacraments but in the whole theological enterprise.

The notion of interpersonal relationship figures large in the interpersonal-encounter model. Three elements stand out in this model. First, an encounter is a "meeting" between two or more persons who experience an I-thou rather than an I-it relationship. ("I-it" means that one person treats the other as an object or a thing rather than as a human being.) Second, the encounter takes place in the present, in the "now." Third, the encounter is a mutual self-giving that recognizes the equality and freedom of both parties. We shall now see how this model is exemplified in the works of two contemporary theologians, Otto Semmelroth and Edward Schillebeeckx.

Otto Semmelroth and the Encounter Model
In his book, *Die Kirche als Ursakrament* (*The Church as Primordial Sacrament*),[17] Senmelroth suggested that each sacrament contains a double or dialogical movement. He called these the sacramental movement and the sacrificial movement. He used the image of a marriage relationship to explain the difference between these two movements.

God's reaching out to encounter man in the sacraments is called the "male movement." That is, God takes the initiative and reaches out to humankind in a gesture of salvation, offering man the opportunity to participate in his Trinitarian life. Semmelroth characterized God's activity as both freely given and effective.

The sacrificial dimension of the encounter was called the "bridal movement." This refers to the attitude and response of the sacramental participants. They react to God's self-gift by offering him in turn their prayers, faith, and commitment. Semmelroth's insistence on the dialogical character of the sacramental relationship between God and humankind is his greatest contribution to the encounter model. The encounter is God himself coming to man. Man's response to this offer is his acceptance of grace, or the actualization of his potential relationship with God.

On the negative side, Semmelroth's use of male-female terminology is certainly out of tune with the current feminist movement. Also, his use of the word "sacrifice" is somewhat ambivalent. Marriage involves more than sacrifice. Furthermore, in its "cultic" sense, the word "sacrifice" means a ritual act of worship or faith that acknowledges God as God. In common usage, however, we think of pain, suffering, and giving up something as our meaning of sacrifice.

The Encounter Model According to Schillebeeckx
Schillebeeckx's major discussion of the encounter model occurs in his text *Christ, the Sacrament of the Encounter with God* (1963).[18] Although the word "encounter" as a sacramental model appears in the title of his book, he did not really construct a sacramentology on the basis of his phenomenology of encounter. He used the model of encounter as a kind of umbrella to gather and organize the classical elements of sacramentology. But the use of this model did permit a new and deeper meaning to emerge from the classical treatises on the subject.

In his use of the encounter model, Schillebeeckx created a new horizon for sacramentology centering on Christ as the sacrament of God, the person-place where the awesome meeting between God and humankind takes place. In his version, the Church is the sacrament of the risen Lord, his continued presence in the world, and the community in which Christ's love for humankind is made historically present and concrete. Christ offers himself to each Christian concretely and immediately in the sacramental events of the Church. But the offer always demands a freely given response of faith, commitment, obedience, and love. Thus, sacramental efficacy involves the *actual outreach* of Christ to us, but the *maximal* or ultimate sacramental reality (grace) demands personal involvement by the recipient.

The interpersonal encounter model just described in the works of Semmelroth and Schillebeeckx also appears in the works of Rahner, Fransen, and other theologians.

Advantages of the Interpersonal-Encounter Model
First, this model reflects more accurately the biblical record of God's dealings with humankind. As in the Scriptures, so in the interpersonal-encounter view of sacraments, an interaction of persons occurs; we have an interrelational event between God and human beings, instead of a mechanical-physical situation like that of the late Scholastic model. Second, interpersonal encounters demand mutual activity, self-giving, freedom, and acceptance. Such a model helps to overcome a purely passive interpretation of sacramental activity, since the individual participants must enter wholeheartedly and faithfully into this meeting with the risen Lord. Third, grace appears not as a thing that can be measured quantitatively or accumulated in that way, but rather as a participated relationship in God's life, manifested in the life of Jesus present in his Church through the power of the Holy Spirit. Grace, then, is characterized as a qualitative relational event that requires personal activity on our part. Sacraments, too, appear as a free and loving exchange of selves between God and the human person.

Deficiencies of the Encounter Model
First, at times the interpersonal-encounter model seems to overemphasize the present moment at the

expense of the past and the future.[19] Granting the importance of the existential moment, no community or person can exist without a meaningful past made present in a ritual celebration, and likewise without an expectation of a meaningful future toward which the community itself is contributing. Second, this model also faces the danger of becoming too individualized; that is, an encounter exclusively between God and me can destroy the mediational character of the sacramental encounter. We must never forget that while the love that God offers us is always personal and immediate to the individual, sacramentally it is mediated in and through the community of the Church as Christ's continued presence in the world. Third, this model may overlook or take for granted the gratuitous or freely given presence of God in the core and depths of humankind. God has already freely bestowed himself upon us through creation, and the sacramental encounter is still another instance of the same free gift of God to man. This freely bestowed presence of God in all creation as well as in the sacraments must not be obscured in the seeming ease and readiness of the sacramental encounter.

CELEBRATION: A NEW SACRAMENTAL MODEL

Introduction
In recent years, it has become a liturgical novelty for the sacramental actions previously described as "saying Mass" or "administering the sacraments" to be called "celebrations."

It should also be observed that the term "celebration" covers a certain variety of functions; not only does it refer to a sacramental action that has a certain solemnity and formality, but it may include diverse functions such as a pontifical Mass in a cathedral or the eucharist celebrated by a small group in a person's home. The word is also applied to ceremonies quite

147

different in character; we speak not only of celebrating a marriage where joy and happiness prevail, but also of celebrating a funeral where the mood is one of sorrow. Obviously then, the word "celebration" as used here in terms of a sacramental model must have a deeper meaning than simply that of surface happiness or merrymaking; it must reach to the depths of faith, where one can find Christian peace and serenity in accord with God's will and in the knowledge of his presence in our life. We think of St. Paul rejoicing in the cross of Christ or in the imprisonment he was suffering, which he said he was offering for Christ's body, the Church. Celebration, then, has a deeper connotation than we ordinarily ascribe to it.

The Life-Context of Celebration
It was noted earlier in our text that God works from *within* as well as from *without*. Therefore, in seeking an integrating model for expressing an understanding of the nature and function of sacrament, we are justified in looking first to human experience and searching out man's fundamental needs as a clue or a pointer to a better understanding of this revealed reality we call "sacrament."

Human Need for Celebration
More than one theologian has pointed out that the need for celebration or festival is a constant in human life. Worgul establishes this need on the basis of an anthropological study of ritual. "[I]t is believed that the celebration model [of sacraments] opens sacramental theological reflection to the vast nourishment available from the anthropological investigation into ritual in general."[20] Vaillancourt establishes the human need for celebration in general, whether secular or religious, on two headings. First, he cites the need to escape from the pressures of everyday life, to draw away from the responsibilities that absorb so much of our time, to

distance ourselves from these in order to grasp the depth and fullness hidden in the everyday and the temporal.[21] The second need cited by Vaillancourt is the need for more profound communion with the social groups that define us. We are, after all, social creatures; our relationships to others define us as a social entity and help to integrate us more fully into the body to which we belong. The very etymology of the word "celebration" coincides with this social need. The Latin noun *celebratio* means a large assembly; the verb *celebrare* means to gather as a throng.[22] Therefore, celebrations are "a release from the servitude of the human condition" and transport us into the world of freedom, gratuitousness, fraternity, and sociableness.[23] They are, he asserts, privileged moments in which we can become aware of the real sources of our life, of what we are beyond the everyday routine, and of what truly gives meaning to our life.

Celebration and Personalization
Working from the behavioral sciences and philosophy, Worgul analyzes further the meaning of celebration as a process of personalization grounded in a dynamism of internalization-externalization.[24] Explaining this, he asserts that the first movement in any celebration is internal. The ritual participants in the celebration, as individuals and community, are turned inward to the source and foundation of the celebration that is the basic reality-event. They tune in to the significance and meaning of the reality-event that is the basis of their celebration and come to realize it as the meaning and the purpose of their coming together. Internalization aims at union, intimacy, and overcoming any barriers of separation or distance. To attain this, participants make use of language, gesture, and symbolic activity.

In the celebration itself, internalization moves toward externalization. As individuals and community, the

149

participants reach out to one another to express the meaning and effect of the experienced reality-event. In the process, the participants become living acting symbols. In and through the participants, the reality-event discloses its depth of meaning. For example, a meaningful eucharist, as celebration of Christ's great loving, paschal surrender for us, ought to move the participants to express their love for one another by praying together and for one another (intercessory prayers), by the sign of peace, by sharing in the common meal of communion, and by extending eucharistic love beyond the ritual celebration by service to the needy, the sick, and so on. In this way, the celebrating community becomes a living vessel of its meaningful treasure.

All of this, the author asserts, affirms a fundamental truth and a condition of human existence. The full meaning of any reality is disclosed and discovered in relation with others. To the extent that they are a being-together, the human person and community reach their fullest comprehension and participation in a reality. Psychological, anthropological, sociological, and philosophical data on ritualization radically support this truth. Psychology cites the importance of others in the development of personality. Sociology presupposes the relational character of human existence. Contemporary philosophy underscores co-existence as a basic principle of human life. In our being with others, the richness of life and love are unfolded. Celebrations, as human events, mirror the dialogical character of human life, in other words, the interplay between individual and community.

Celebrations and the "Common Man"
Moving more explicitly to man's need for religious celebrations, Piet Fransen, in an excellent discussion of "sacraments as celebrations," adverts to the lived ex-

perience of "the common man" to justify his support for the need of sacraments to be viewed as celebrations.[25] Commenting on the religious attitudes of the farmers in the villages and the workers in the industrial centers of France, he notes that their faith is more direct in its expression (that is, not so articulate and reflexive or intellectual), more deeply embedded in traditional attitudes, especially family traditions, and also more emotional and corporate than the generally reserved, rational, and reflexive faith of the intellectual elite. The spontaneous way to express their faith is the celebration of a feast. Their faith is awakened, he maintains, by the festive character of baptism, the traditional celebrations of the solemn or first communion, by marriages, burials, and liturgical feasts such as Christmas. These are all festive occasions that spontaneously overflow into the life of the family and the community. They are rooted in the cultural and religious past and are part of a precious human and communal lore in which festive clothing, special meals, dances, fairs, pageants, and other more or less secular forms of celebration are intermingled with and support the faith celebration. Such festive celebrations, he believes, so different from the dreary and depressing atmosphere of daily life, witness to an obscure but tenacious hope for salvation.

Family, geographical, cultural, and religious roots are very important. While the West generally celebrates Christmas as a family occasion, the Russian and Greek Orthodox celebrate Easter as the great popular and religious feast. The Eastern churches in general recognize a greater festive quality to their liturgical celebrations than do the churches of the West. The liturgy on earth is viewed as the symbolic participation in the unique and eternal heavenly liturgy.

The same need for festive celebration by the common people, Fransen observes, is noted among the people of the so-called Third World, in contrast to our rational, individualistic Western culture. Their religious traditions combine various emotional, imaginative, rhythmic, and even rational aspects of human experience into one festive celebration. He draws upon his experience in Africa, where he witnessed the importance of the festive character of liturgy as evidenced in the music, dancing, and lively participation of the people in their native religious celebrations.

Still another group in the Church that seems to have rediscovered the value of the festive character of our faith is modern youth. Youth masses with guitar and music, rhythmic songs, and dance manifest a deep hunger for a more spontaneous, joyful, and truly liberated form of faith-life.

In all of these examples of human experience, Fransen sees a kind of verification for the human need of celebration in ritual. The people of God, he maintains, meet God through beauty, the beauty of hymns and gestures, of vestments and music. Scripture readings should be chosen with this pastoral concern in view. Artists and poets should be invited to create in our vernacular languages the same beauty of expression that the monks produced in the Gregorian Chant. There is no true celebration without true beauty and without a symbolic unity of expression in which all the normal human feelings and insights are recognized and manifested. Religion indeed addresses the whole person, not only the intellect.

Characteristics of Celebration
It is not easy to construct an all-embracing definition of the human experience we call "celebration." Worgul attempts to give us a descriptive definition of human celebration that he later applies to the sacraments as Christian celebrations. For him, "a celebration is a

communal activity by which a community manifests, symbolizes, and makes present to their individual selves and the members of the community the reality of a joyful, consoling, enriching reality-event."[26] According to Worgul, his definition presents celebration both as a symbol and a model. A celebration points to a reality and makes it present without being identical to the reality. This is its symbolic function. Insofar as it also structures reality into a particular form or order so that a particular reality-event can be understood, celebration then also becomes a model.

All celebrations are a kind of ritual that engages two or more people, generally enough people to constitute a true community. Celebrations are ways of gathering together and growing together by common symbolizing and making-present a definite reality-event. Worgul cites an example of a twenty-fifth wedding anniversary celebration. The reality-event being celebrated is twenty-five years of shared life and love. Celebration with its various elements of party, song, dances, family, friends, and stories allows the shared life and love of the anniversary couple to become more real to them as well as to the gathered community. The original event of the marriage is what he means by the charter-event or reality-event that is being celebrated. This is obviously the *sine qua non* for the celebration.

He proceeds to discuss a threefold time dimension for celebrations, much as Thomas Aquinas did for the sacraments.[27] Celebrations may be said to have a common past, a present reality, and a future expectation. The celebration of a common past (in this case a wedding) suggests a further aspect of celebrations, that is, that generally they are repeated on a more or less regular basis. Through this repetition, a bond is maintained with the original event, and the community is strengthened by a shared identity among its members.

Families celebrate birthdays. Religious communities celebrate the feast and significant events of their founder. Nations celebrate regularly their founding date (e.g., our July Fourth). All of these various celebrations take the participants back to their origins, in which they find their common identity, and as a consequence, find a new solidarity among themselves.

In the present moment, a given celebration in a certain way makes the original event come to life again. Identity with the past is maintained, and the bond of community is sustained. Certainly the anniversary celebrants who have been married 25 years may be moved through the celebration to reflect upon their life together through 25 years of testing, sacrifice, and fidelity, and thus deepen and strengthen this relationship.

Furthermore, the present moment of a celebration may be a *kairos*, that is, a critical opportunity, a blessed time, a time of choice. In the case of the wedding celebrants, they generally renew their commitment to one another for the future and thus reinforce the original reality-event of their marriage. On a larger scale, such as a national celebration of its beginnings, the whole nation may be called to renew its commitment to the original ideals of the founding fathers. A celebration of the charter-event upon which the nation's identity rests may also serve to galvanize the present generation to greater national effort in helping to preserve and, if necessary, defend the nation against threats to its autonomy.

Finally, celebrations are more than a memory and a present reenactment of the past; they are also future-oriented, marked with an expectation or hope to celebrate again. The happily married couple celebrating their twenty-fifth anniversary will look forward to many future anniversary celebrations.

154

The Sacraments as Christian Celebrations

Worgul's Approach

Applying his definition of general celebration to the Christian sacraments, Worgul selects three principal features that identify sacraments as celebrations. These three features he describes as: (1) a way of being together (community); (2) a manifestation and symbolic activity; and (3) a reality-event as a given. At this point, he repeats his own definition of sacraments as "symbols arising from the ministry of Jesus, continued in and through the Church, which when received in faith, are encounters with God, Father, Son, and Holy Spirit."[28]

Sacraments as Ecclesial Acts: First of all, sacraments are ecclesial or community acts; they are always sacraments of and through the Church. This means the entire community, the *koinonia*, the brotherhood, a way of being together in Christ. Sacraments are symbolic activities of the ecclesial Christian community and community patterns of behavior in which the nature of the community is expressed and realized. The Church is God's gathered people, for he is the agent of this community. Through the gathered community, then, the individual experiences "salvation," for the church fellowship, or *ecclesia*, is also the mediation and concurrently the effect of grace.

Sacraments as Symbolic Activities: Sacraments express and realize in ritual form the presence of the living God offering himself to the community; at the same time, they are the community's acceptance of God's love in their act of worship. Sacraments are symbolic realities—activities or modes of expression that engage the totality of the participants, that is, their cognitive, volitional, emotional, and physical powers.

Furthermore, sacraments are performative acts. People

155

"do" sacraments. Precisely as ritual activities, sacraments make present the offer of God's love. Community ritual activities enable the participants to experience again the power of the death and resurrection of Christ (the charter event of Christianity) and to be conformed to the meaning of this event. The participants are united with Christ through the power of the Spirit in Christ's worship of and obedience to the Father. Such union with the Trinity is exactly what grace and salvation are all about.

Sacraments as Celebrations of a Central Reality-Event: Grounding the entire sacramental celebration is the reality-event of the Son of God's entrance into human history, his gathering of a people to himself, his death-resurrection Passover, and his continued presence among them in the power of the Spirit, the very personification of Christ's love for his people. Sacraments, then, are celebrations of this joyful, consoling, fulfilling charter-event. Christ himself is the cause of the sacramental celebration, which aims at a deeper union of the participants with himself and with one another.

Vaillancourt's Approach
In his discussion of sacramental celebrations, Vaillancourt stresses the primacy of the assembly as the locus of the celebration. In fact, the strengthening of community, as he sees it, is one of the principal goals of these ritual celebrations. They exist, he maintains, not so much to worship God, but rather to welcome him into the midst of the community and to recall the divine interventions in human history, which in turn generate Christian community (cf. Fransen's rather different view in the next section). He sees a deeply felt need for the community to be motivated toward a constant growth in togetherness and a need to participate

as actively as possible in the ongoing life of the community.

Fransen's Approach

After noting that the English word "celebrate" can mean "to make famous," "to extol," and to "publish abroad," Fransen proceeds to discuss religious celebration or sacrament by highlighting two points. First, he sees it primarily as a public and ritual act of worship, a liturgy. Within this description, he emphasizes that it is a corporate or joint activity of the ecclesial community directed primarily toward God, Christ, and the saints. He views the sacramental celebrations in continuity with the Hebrew notion of worship and sacrifice as enacting a *service* of praise and adoration. Thus his view is in contrast with Vaillancourt's emphasis on sacraments as God's gifts to us rather than our rendition of service or praise to him.

The second point stressed by Fransen is the joyful dimension of celebration. The joy that should dominate the celebration of the sacraments is a joy over the good news of the gospel, the object of our faith and hope. It is joy too about God's "glory," which in biblical terms means the visible manifestation of God's majesty, love, and mercy. Thus genuine human worship manifests, reveals, and witnesses to God's glory.

Fransen goes to some length to describe further what he means by Christian joy in the context of the sacramental celebration. Joy for him is not a maudlin or cheap superficial emotion; true to human experience, joy is always intermingled with sorrow or, as he puts it, a laugh with a tear. Human existence has a depth dimension of futility, insecurity, and tragedy. It cannot be without pain and suffering, and so we cannot conceal these aspects of reality behind naive songs about happiness, even on the most festive occasions.

157

The greatest artistic creations in music, sculpture, drama, and poetry, he points out, are those in which human life is truly celebrated, its sorrows as well as its joys.

On a more theological plane, he points to the co-existence of a theology of the "cross" along with a theology of "glory." The Son of God saved us by emptying himself unto humiliation and death (Phil. 2:5ff.). Therefore, the Christian too is summoned to follow Jesus in his self-emptying (*kenosis*) in order to share the triumph of his resurrection. The Christian life exists in a sort of tension between the constant need for conversion and self-improvement, and the joy of present and future union with Christ.

Object of Sacramental Celebrations

Exactly what is it that we celebrate in the sacraments? In a way, our answers necessarily will reflect what we said in the previous two chapters about their proclamatory and actualizing functions. Nevertheless, our present discussion of the objective sacramental celebration will highlight the personal and existential qualities of the celebrational model for sacraments.

Since every celebration has a common past, present, and future, we will gather our reflections under the temporal headings of *anamnesis* (memorial or remembrance), *kairos* (present moment of grace), and *eschaton* (the future or End Time). In using these three time categories, we are on solid biblical, patristic, and Scholastic grounds. Thomas Aquinas himself spoke of this threefold time dimension in terms of the significative power of sacraments as commemorative signs, demonstrative signs, and prognostic or prefiguring signs.[29] Thus sacramental celebrations are truly immersed in time; they originate in the past, transpire in the present, and yearn for the future.

Anamnesis (Remembrance)

The basis of any celebration is the reality-event itself.
For Christians, this primordial event is, of course, the
Passover mystery of Jesus, his death-resurrection and
sending of the Spirit. Thomas Aquinas expressed a
similar thought when he said that all the sacraments
go back to the passion of Christ as their source of
power. Today, in the light of contemporary biblical
studies, we would want to locate the saving Passover
of Jesus within the total framework of salvation history; this would lead us to say that, in a way, all of
God's interventions for mankind—including creation,
the formation of Israel especially through the Exodus,
the fullness of revelation in Jesus, and his public
ministry among mankind—are crowned with the
paschal mystery of Jesus and capsulated in our sacramental celebrations. Therefore, sacraments celebrate
the memorial of God's saving deeds for humankind,
but especially the great salvation event of Jesus' passage through death to risen life. It is to this premier
saving event that we owe the existence of the Church,
the sacraments, and grace. Without this charter event,
there would be nothing to celebrate; there would be no
reason for us to gather in sacramental assembly.

The *Kairos* or Present Actuality of Sacraments

Celebrations of Faith: It goes without saying that in any
given moment of sacramental celebration, the govern-
ing spirit of the assembly must be the attitude of faith.
Sacraments are first of all celebrations of our Christian
faith, both as individuals and as community. For it is
the supernatural gift of faith that moves us as individuals into the assembly of believers to express and
ratify a common belief in God, and in what he has
done for us in the past and promises to do in the future (cf. our public proclamation of the "creed" at our
Sunday eucharist). When we gather as celebrators of

liturgy, we gather first of all as an assembly of faith. We remember that we are the heirs of a tradition of faith to which we were committed at the time of our baptism and confirmation. It is this inner attitude of faith that must now characterize our intellectual and emotional surrender to the moment of sacramental encounter, the celebration of Christ's risen presence among us.

Celebrations of the Paschal Mystery: As a gathered community of faith, we celebrate first of all the actual presence in mystery of the saving Passover of our founder Jesus Christ. As we explained in Chapter 5, we are not only commemorating a past event when we celebrate the death and resurrection of Jesus, but as heirs of the Hebrew tradition of "memorial,"[30] we are celebrating a present reality, for somehow the saving deeds of Jesus in the past are now made present so that we can enter into them, relive them, and have communion with the Christ who has died and is gloriously risen for us. The paschal mystery, in short, is not just an event locked in the past; it is also an event actualized in the present by every sacrament, especially baptism and the eucharist. Jesus' saving Passover, after all, is the source of our salvation; it is the grounding of our celebration of every sacrament. By God's mysterious providence, this saving mystery becomes actually present under symbols so that we may experience it, make contact with it, and accept the saving and loving presence of the Christ who has given himself totally for us. Every sacrament, therefore, is not merely a commemoration of the past, but an actual reliving or reenactment of the source of our salvation. The charter-event of our salvation becomes present for us in every sacrament in different ways, so that by giving ourselves unreservedly to this mystery, we may experience the liberating presence of Christ in our lives both as community and as individuals.

The Inner Presence of God in Grace: The fruit of the Passover mystery of Jesus as experienced in our present sacramental celebrations takes the form of God's presence to us as *grace*. It is this aspect of celebration that is particularly emphasized by Fransen.[31] Grace, he reminds us, is not merely a help or a means to a better life. It is actual union with God in Trinity: Father, Son, and Holy Spirit. Through the sacramental effects of grace, God makes himself present to us in a most special way as the great fruit of the paschal mystery of Jesus, which unites us to the inner life of God. Thus he becomes the inner voice or the inner depth of our being. Faith enables us to be conscious of this nearness of God to ourselves as well as to our neighbor. The paschal mystery bears its fruit in our life as we become conscious of our intimate association with the God to whom Christ has come to unite us. We think of John 14:23, where the Gospel writer speaks of the Father and the Son taking up their dwelling in the person of the just. This is indeed cause for celebration as we witness joyfully and confidently to the life that is in us, a life that is so holy and pure that to know about it means also to know about our own indignity and sinfulness. We celebrate in joy his loving nearness, the abundance of his gifts, the fidelity of his inner words, the mercy of his forgiveness. We celebrate the kingdom of God within us. Sacraments then are truly celebrations of our life as rooted in God.

We might call this approach to the sacraments a contemplative and festive one. It is inevitably characterized by an intense feeling of joy, freedom, and fullness; in this perspective, every form of magic is thoroughly banished.

The presence of God in us in grace, however, is not purely an individual experience. The Spirit in us prompts us to recognize God as the inner sanctuary of others as well, for God is in all his creatures in one way or another. He is the inner power of the universe, the inner soul of the cosmos and its history, a view already initiated by the great Franciscan theologians of the Middle Ages. Even for the contemporary Jew, God's glory is manifested as the *shekinah* ("indwelling" or "presence") realized primarily in man.

Celebration of Self-Realization: Sacraments, then, can be viewed as celebrating what we truly are, human beings endowed with a spiritual nature capable of being elevated to a union with God in grace. We celebrate our human dignity as creatures of intellect and freedom, of joy, and of love. We celebrate that we have been created in God's image and likeness and therefore have an intrinsic dignity. We celebrate the God that is *within* as well as *without*. For by creating us as spiritual as well as bodily creatures, God has endowed us with the potential to be raised to something beyond ourselves, to accomplish a self-transcendence with the help of his grace.

In this view of celebration as a realization of God's presence within us in grace, a new dimension of understanding is given to the efficacy of the sacraments. Efficacy does not necessarily have the mechanical meaning of producing something new. In and through our festive acknowledgement in faith and hope of God's ineffable inner presence, we actualize and realize it under the graceful attraction of that inner presence. This kind of sacramental efficacy would look more like a wonderful form of self-realization, where, of course, the deepest self is God himself behind and within our own inner self. In the celebration of the sacraments, the image of God in which we have been created would thus expand, ripen, blossom, and come to greater actualization. It would be an efficacy of growth, of inner liberation and joy, the joy that modern Christianity so often lacks. Truly then, the presence of God as Father, Son, and Spirit present to us in a special way through grace is cause for sacramental celebration.

Celebration of Our Ecclesial Identity: As we have indicated, grace is not only an individual gift, but a gift to the whole community. Sacraments, particularly through their first effect, the *res et sacramentum*, establish us in a special relationship to the Church community. We are never more "Church" than when we assemble to celebrate the sacraments. Thus at their very roots, sacraments are celebrations of our community in Christ. They are celebrations that help to sustain our identity as members of a faith community.

As such, sacramental celebrations impel us to a more active commitment to the community in which we meet the risen Christ and are sustained and reinforced by the celebration of his paschal mystery. When we proclaim our creed (in Latin *symbolum fidei*—"symbol of faith") in the eucharist, through our acclamations, or in sharing any of the other sacraments, we are reacting to the gracious outreach of the saving Christ and his love. Sacraments then, are truly celebrations of our ecclesial togetherness in the life of Christ united by his Spirit.

Celebrations of a New World of Meaning: Today we think of the world in terms of meaning. However, contrary to the thought of some people, meaning is not a purely subjective reality, but is first a given aspect of reality. It belongs to being as such and manifests itself in the mutual relationships of those beings with one another. Beings are within the world what they are for themselves and for others. We become quite conscious of this givenness when we ignore or distort it, as in the case of the nature and function of marriage. No authentic life can be founded on a lie.

Theologically, we can say further that the deepest meaning of beings is what they are in God's creative providence and care. This is not a static notion of human nature and natural law, but allows for the fact that human beings may change and develop continuously. The God-given meaning, therefore, is not a static reality, given once for all, but a dynamic aspect of reality in terms of our human history.

If God is the ultimate source of meaning, there is also room for our own creative spontaneity in creating meaning. Our own human perception (together with its content) is, according to Schillebeeckx, "raised above purely sensory relativity and taken in the direction of the spiritual meaning of reality. It therefore refers externally, as in signs, to reality itself, which, as such, only has meaning for the human spirit. In this sense, *man himself fashions the signifying function* that the content of his perception has with regard to reality and makes this content a referential sign."[32] Again he writes:

"Partly through sensory perception, man opens himself up to the mystery of reality, to the metaphysical being which is prior to and is offered to man's ontological sense—that is, to his *logos* [interpretative reason], which *makes* being *appear* and thus *establishes meaning* . . . *The phenomenal* is the *sign* of reality. . . . Explicit knowledge of reality is therefore a complex unity, in which an *active* openness to what communicates itself as reality is accompanied by a *giving of meaning*. What in fact shows itself to me, however, also acts as a norm for the meaning I give to the reality."[33]

Besides the individual's "giving of meaning," Piet Fransen also sees a social dimension to this process. Meaning is created in the many ways we relate ourselves freely and creatively to others in the continuous flow of history. We create meaning together with others of our community as we create language, the

164

expression of meaning, and as we create ever-changing patterns of behavior, the bearers of meaning.

While there can be a tension between the given and the spontaneously creatively accepted aspect of meaning, the basic cause of this tension is sin, the refusal to accept God's own meaning. Meaning itself possesses an inner dynamism toward unity, harmony, and integration.

When God establishes his divine presence in us and in the community of men, he is to be recognized as our primary source of meaning, the meaning given to us in Christ. This meaning was prepared for many centuries of Old Testament history, especially by the prophets; fundamentally, once and for all, it was given in the coming of Christ and expressed in language and patterns of behavior in the teaching and life of Jesus. This Christian meaning was entrusted to the Church. It is continuously being realized, perfected, and reformed by the inner instinct of the Holy Spirit.

On the other hand, God reaches us as human beings who have free access to him. We accept God's meaning in the obedience of faith, not mechanically or passively, but creatively in love. We accept God's meaning as ours in faith, hope, and love.

If we now look at the sacraments as celebrations of our Christian life, we see them as real sources of meaning in the dialectic sense that we have explained. In the sacraments, God is reaching toward us through Christ and his Spirit. The meaning of the sacraments, according to ancient tradition, is expressed and accepted in the faith of the Church. The community of the Church keeps alive the original meaning of the sacraments as sources of salvation and redemption. In their celebration, we assimilate and identify ourselves with their God-given meaning. That is why Thomas Aquinas insisted on the importance of faith in the reception of the sacraments. It is in our Christian faith that we grasp the meaning God has revealed to us.

The Church, however, recognizes a certain evolution or development in the meaning of the sacraments. They are not dead symbols. They are alive and open to the needs of men. Therefore, the church adapts its rites to the needs of the Christian people. The sacraments are the fundamental expressions of our communion in the Church. The meaning that they impart, therefore, structures our whole Christian life. In other words, sacraments are the visible and ecclesial expressions of the God-given meaning, which was founded in God's graceful presence and accepted by the Church.

Fransen concludes his article in the following summarization: "The model of celebration manifests the unity and harmony of the new life in grace we are confessing in the Symbols (the creeds), accepting in the celebration of the sacraments, and to which we are finally committing ourselves for our further life in Christ. Celebration adds a nuance of freedom, joy, and communion. Meaning is precisely realized in freedom and joy, thanksgiving and praise, humble creativity, and always together."[34]

Sacramental Celebrations and the Future
Just as the Hebrew traditions always looked to the future—for example, the celebrations of the exodus prepared Israel for an even greater liberation in the future—so the Christian sacraments, the liturgy of Christ's Church, are not only anchored in the past and the present, but also lead us into the future. They are eschatological; that is, they are directed ultimately to leading us into the final Kingdom of God, the new heavens and the new earth. Thomas Aquinas called the sacraments a promise of future glory. We must try to recover a sense of this future orientation of sacramental celebration.

166

Just as all human celebrations are marked with an expectation or hope to celebrate again, so the sacraments envision as valuable and meaningful for the future the continuing celebration of the Passover mystery of Christ.

The liturgy itself includes this three-dimensional aspect of past, present, and future; for example, in the Midnight Mass of Christmas we pray: "Lord, you made this holy night resplendent with the brilliance of the true light. Grant that, being enlightened here below by the revelation of this mystery, we may taste its joy to the full in heaven." Thus, the liturgy transports us into this future world as it speaks of heaven and all that goes with it. The primitive Church was especially caught up with the notion of an imminent *parousia*—that is, the final coming of Christ in the very near future—to usher in the definitive stage of the Kingdom. When this did not happen, the Church began to look more and more to the past and the present as the source of its hope for a more distant ultimate realization of its expectations. Today, people feel ill at ease with the gospel and liturgical allusions to the final coming of Christ. We need to formulate a new language for presenting and making vividly real this dimension of eschatological or futuristic expectation.

In the Lord's Prayer, we pray "may your Kingdom come"; but the full impact of the meaning of what we are saying scarcely strikes home. Every movement needs a goal or purpose, and we need to realize that our ultimate goal and purpose is final union with God in heaven. Thus, the sacraments as the public celebrations of our faith community need to highlight and express as clearly as possible our hope in the future. The theology of the risen Christ preceding us to the Father (cf. Moltmann[35]) is meant to turn our vision precisely in the direction of the future. A great part of Marxism's appeal is precisely its promises for the future. We need to realize that Christianity too is not only built on the past, but also grounded on the promise of an ultimate future with God and with one another. Sacraments should inspire us not only to hope for this future, but to help bring it about.

Just as so many of the Gospel parables, such as the wedding feast or the messianic banquet (the never-ending celebration of joy with God in heaven), emphasized the future to which Christ is leading us, so we must become more aware of the futuristic promise and joyful hope that the sacraments intend to give us. As we affirm joyfully in our liturgy: "Christ has died, Christ is risen, Christ will come again."

Evaluation of the Celebration Model
George Worgul evaluates the celebration model of sacraments by articulating its advantages and its possible deficiencies.[36] He compares the celebration model with the models summarized previously in this chapter. First, without denying the positive value of the interpersonal-encounter model, the celebration model corrects the former's telescoping of time and individualistic tendencies. The encounter model, he contends, does not always sufficiently take into account the three temporal modes of past, present, and future as we have specified them. These temporal modes of sacramental celebrations link the Christian community to human history. The past dimension links the community to its origins and identity. The present dimension sustains the community in the here and now. The future dimension establishes the reality-event of God's love as the hoped for future and the evaluative principle of ecclesial planning and performance.

Furthermore, whereas the encounter model may tend to an individualistic conception of sacraments as a meeting between Christ and the individual, the celebration model emphasizes sacraments as communal ritual activities. They are ecclesial in nature, while including the active role of the individuals who comprise the community.

Moreover, the celebration model corrects the imbalance of the late Scholastic model of sacraments as a kind of mechanistic or physical operation. Celebrations are human behavior; they operate in the realm of human symbolic activity. Celebration employs the idiom of persons rather than things to understand the interaction of God and humankind in ritual activity.

Finally, in comparison to Casel's mystery-presence theory, the celebration model seems better adapted to explain the presence of God in the sacramental activity of the community. The celebration model relies on and appeals to the data on ritual in general to substantiate its claims. In short, it relies on the acceptance of Christian ritual as a realization or actualization of the past interventions of God in human history, as well as an eschatological orientation toward the fullness of the Kingdom.

On the negative side, the celebration model contains a danger implicit in sacramentology *per se*. Celebration presupposes faith or belief in a reality-event. The celebration model rises or falls on a faithful commitment to the reality-event of the Christian God as ground and givenness of sacraments. If commitment to the meaning of this reality-event is absent from sacramental celebrations, they will be empty expressions. Without faith, sacraments rapidly degenerate into magic and eventual oblivion.

In summary, according to Worgul, among the four models proposed for sacraments in this chapter, the celebration model seems best to reflect the dynamism of a reconstructed sacramentology. Sacraments are not things, but ritual activities that follow the constitutive structures of ritual in general. The celebration model corresponds to the data supporting our theological claims about sacraments in general. Celebrations begin with common human experience; they involve both the individual and community. Further, celebration is concerned with the transmission and evaluation of meaning. They are symbolic activities, performative and penetrating. Only a model open to expressing the full depths of reality can evoke the discovery of God's mysterious love and self-gift to humankind. Celebration is open to this task and in many ways attains this goal.

Pastoral Observations
Concluding our presentation of celebration as a new model for understanding sacraments, it seems appropriate to take notice of the needs of the people in planning and carrying out sacramental celebrations. The Second Vatican Council and the Sacred Congregation for Worship and Sacraments seem to have taken this into account in providing different forms of celebration, for example, for baptism and reconciliation, special provision for children's Masses, and so on. For baptism, different forms of celebration exist for infants and adults (RCIA, Rite of Christian Initiation of Adults). For reconciliation, there is provision for a private celebration of the sacrament between priest and penitent, communal celebration with private confession of sin, and general absolution. Anointing of the sick may be given privately or communally. Perhaps too, we need various types of celebration for other sacraments such as marriage, and greater variations in the eucharistic ritual. This is because it is difficult to make explicit all the functions and dimensions of one and the same sacrament in a given celebration. Thus one celebration of the eucharist can truly bring out the communion already existing among Christians, while another can emphasize the communion still to be achieved. Some celebrations can emphasize the func-

tion of proclamation, while others can emphasize the function of celebration. Thus we need a variety of forms to express the involvement of Christ, the Church, and the individual with varying degrees of emphasis.

At the same time, we may note that the celebration model of sacraments does not preclude their value as proclamations or actualizations of the saving presence and activity of Christ. All three functions may come together simultaneously, at least at times, but generally, one or the other will be highlighted. The function of proclamation, for example, is extremely important in explaining what the celebration is all about and in galvanizing the community to an active attestation of communal faith.

Finally we need to recall that, as Avery Dulles pointed out in *Models of the Church*, one model alone cannot exhaust the complex realities of Revelation (in this case, the Church). The same is true of sacraments; we need several models to complement one another, to correct one another, and to express the full, rich reality of what sacraments are. As Fransen suggested, sacraments refer to many activities such as causing, being present, encountering, worshiping, confessing, and praising. This is the challenge of sacramentology that faces theologians of the future—to seek out and elaborate models for sacraments that will do full justice to their profound reality and function.

NOTES

1. Avery Dulles, *Models of the Church* (New York: Doubleday, 1974).

2. Bernard Lonergan, S.J., *Method in Theology* (New York: Herder & Herder, 1972)

3. Dulles, *op. cit.*, pp. 22–23; cf. also M. McLain, "On Theological Models," *Harvard Theological Review* 62 (1969)

155–188; E. Cousins, "Models and the Future of Theology," *Continuum* 76 (1969) 78–92; and E. Lepin, "Denkmodelle des Glaubens," *Zeitschrift für Theologie und Kirche* 16 (1969) 210– 44. See for more general studies on this topic, *The Rules of the Game, Cross-disciplinary Essays on Models*, ed. Teodor Shanin (London: Tavistock, 1972), esp. pp. 1–22; and Max Black, *Models and Metaphors*, (Ithaca, N.Y.: Cornell University Press, 1962).

4. For much of the following material, I am indebted to George S. Worgul, Jr. *From Magic to Metaphor* (New York: Paulist Press, 1980), pp. 203–17.

5. Edward Schillebeeckx, *Christ, the Sacrament of the Encounter with God* (New York: Sheed & Ward, 1963) pp. 92–95.

6. Odo Casel, *The Mystery of Christian Worship*, trans. from the German, ed. Burkhard Neunheuser (Westminster, Md.: Newman Press, 1962), p. 54.

7. Ibid., p. 141.

8. Ibid., p. 142.

9. Ibid., p. 152; emphasis added.

10. Ibid., p. 154.

11. Ibid., p. 158.

12. J. H. Nicolas, "Reactualization des mystères Redempteurs dans et par les sacrements," *Revue Thomiste* (Jan.-March 1958) 20 (quoted in *Worship* 34:3 [1960] 165). Cf. also Piet Fransen's evaluation, "Sacraments as Celebrations," *Irish Theological Quarterly*, 43:3 (1976) 160.

13. Cf. Ernst Käsemann, *Commentary on Romans*, trans. Geoffrey W. Bromiley (Grand Rapids, Mich.: Eerdmans, 1980) p. 6, commenting on the introduction to the letter, where Paul calls himself an apostle selected or called by Christ for the service of the gospel. Käsemann notes: "The prophetic calling appears now in an *apocalyptic* perspective." We think of Paul's concern for the parousia or final coming of Christ (esp. 1 & 2 Thes.); the promise or pledge of our own resurrection because of Christ's resurrection and installation as Lord of the universe (e.g., 1 Cor. 15); his teaching on virginity as an

eschatological vocation, one that reminds others of the coming of the Kingdom (1 Cor. 7); the eucharist as proclaiming the Lord's death "until he comes" (1 Cor. 11:26); and of course a multitude of references too many to mention here. Käsemann, further, captions a whole section of Romans (5:1–8:39) as "The Righteousness of Faith as a Reality of *Eschatological* Freedom." Without question, Paul bears the stamp of eschatological preacher, always oriented to the End Time, where all things will be redirected to the Father under the headship of Christ (cf. Eph. 1:10).

14. Cf. John Macquarrie, *An Existentialist Theology* (New York: Harper & Row, 1965), pp. 11ff.

15. Ibid. (an interpretation or paraphrase of Rudolf Bultmann's approach), p. 230.

16. Ibid., p. 14.

16a. Martin Buber, *I and Thou*, 2nd ed., trans. Ronald G. Smith (New York: Scribner's, 1958), pp. 3–34.

17. Otto Semmelroth, S.J., *Die Kirche als Ursakrament* (Franfurt, 1952).

18. Op. cit.

19. According to Worgul, op. cit., p. 212.

20. Worgul, *op. cit.*, p. 213. His study of the socio-anthropological data on ritual is found on pp. 70–105.

21. Raymond Vaillancourt, *Toward a Renewal of Sacramental Theology*, trans. Matthew J. O'Connell (Collegeville, Minn.: The Liturgical Press, 1979), p. 103.

22. Cf. *Oxford Latin Dictionary*, Fascicle II (Oxford: Clarendon Press, 1969), p. 293.

23. Vaillancourt, *op. cit.*, pp. 103, 104.

24. Worgul, *op. cit.*, p. 217.

25. Piet Fransen, "Sacraments as Celebrations," *Irish Theological Quarterly* 43:3 (1976) 151–70 (esp. for this point, pp. 163–66).

26. Worgul, op. cit., p. 213.

27. Cf. S.T., 60, 3.

28. Worgul, op. cit., p. 218.

29. S.T. III, 60, 3.

30. Cf. Max Thurian, *The Eucharistic Memorial* (Richmond: John Knox Press, Vol. I, 1960; Vol. II, 1961). The first volume discusses in detail the *realistic* meaning of *memorial* (*Zikka-ron*) for the Hebrews. Thurian then applies this understanding to Jesus' use of the word at the Last Supper. "Do this as a *memorial* for me." So too, the other sacraments "actualize" the original charter event from which they are ultimately derived: the paschal mystery. Cf. Chapter 5 of this book.

31. Fransen, op. cit., pp. 166f.

32. Edward Schillebeeckx, *The Eucharist* (New York: Sheed & Ward, 1968), p. 146. Emphasis added.

33. Ibid., pp. 147–48.

34. Fransen, op. cit., p. 170.

35. J. Moltmann, *Theology of Hope* (New York: Harper and Row, 1967), trans. J.W. Leitch. For a further discussion of his theology, cf. J.P. Schanz, *A Theology of Community* (Washington, D.C.: University Press of America, 1977), pp. 285–99.

36. Worgul, op. cit., pp. 220f.

174

Selected Readings

GENERAL WORKS

Berkouwer, Gerrit. *The Sacraments*, trans. Hugo Bekker (Grand Rapids, Mich.: Eerdmans, 1969).

Burns, Patout J. (S.J.). "Seminar on Church and Sacraments: Summary," *Catholic Theological Society of America Proceedings* 32 (1977), pp. 195–97.

———. "Seminar on the Church and Sacraments: Why the Sacraments," *Catholic Theological Society of America Proceedings* 33 (1978), pp. 199–202.

Cooke, Bernard. *Ministry to Word and Sacraments: History and Theology* (Philadelphia: Fortress Press, 1976).

Constitution on the Sacred Liturgy, Vatican II (AAS, Vol. 56, No. 2, Feb. 15, 1964). Trans. in Austin Flannery, *Documents of Vatican II* (Grand Rapids, Mich.: Eerdmans, 1975), pp. 1–37.

Didier, R. *Les sacrements de la foi* (Paris: Le Centurion, 1975).

Dyer, George. (ed.). "Design for American Worship," *Chicago Studies* 16:1 (1977), entire volume of articles.

Eigo, Francis A. (O.S.A.) (ed.). *The Sacraments: God's Love and Mercy Actualized* (Villanova, Pa.: Villanova University Press, 1979).

Flannery, Austin P. (ed.). *Documents of Vatican II* (Grand Rapids, Mich.: Eerdmans, 1975).

Granfield, Patrick (O.S.B.). "Seminar on Church and Sacraments: Summary," *Catholic Theological Society of America Proceedings* 31 (1976), pp. 133–42.

Guzie, Tad. *The Book of Sacramental Basics* (New York: Paulist Press, 1981).

Hellwig, Monika. *The Meaning of the Sacraments* (Dayton, Ohio: Pflaum, 1972).

Höfer, Josef and Karl Rahner (eds.). "Sakrament," in *Lexikon für Theologie und Kirche*, Vol. 9 (Freiburg: Herder, 1964), 2nd ed., pp. 218–31, 239–43.

Kavanagh, Aidan. "Sacrament as an Act of Service," *Worship* 39 (1965), pp. 89–96.

Keefe, D. "Toward a Renewal of Sacramental Theology," *The Thomist* 44 (1980), pp. 357–71.

Kiesling, Christopher (O.P.). "How Many Sacraments," *Worship* 44 (1970), pp. 268–76.

Küng, Hans (ed.). *The Sacraments: An Ecumenical Dilemma*, *Concilium*, Vol. 24 (New York: Paulist Press, 1966).

Leeming, Bernard. *Principles of Sacramental Theology* (London: Longmans, 1960), 2nd ed.

Lonergan, Bernard, J.F. (S.J.). *Method in Theology* (New York: Herder & Herder, 1972).

Martos, Joseph. *Doors to the Sacred: A Historical Introduction to Sacraments in the Catholic Church* (New York: Doubleday, 1981).

McCauley, George. *Sacraments for Secular Man* (New York: Herder & Herder, 1969).

McManus, Fred. "The Sacraments of the Church," *Chicago Studies* 15 (1976), pp. 349–71.

Ong, Walter. "Catholic Theology Now," *Theology Digest* 23:4 (1975), pp. 338–46.

Osborne, K.R. "Sacramental Theology" (pp. 591ff.) and "Sacraments, Theology of" (pp. 594–96), in *New Catholic Encyclopedia*, Supplement (1979).

Pannikar, Raimundo, "Man as a Ritual Being," *Chicago Studies* 16:1 (1977), pp. 5–28.

———. *Worship and Secular Man* (Maryknoll, N.Y.: Orbis, 1973).

Power, David N. "Unripe Grapes: The Critical Function of Liturgical Theology," *Worship* 52:5 (1978), pp. 386–99.

Powers, Joseph. *Spirit and Sacrament: The Humanizing Experience* (New York: Seabury Press, 1973).

Rahner, Karl. *Meditations on the Sacraments* (New York: Seabury Press, Crossroad Books), 1978.

Rondet, H. *La vie sacramentaire* (Paris: Fayard, 1972).

"Sacramental ministry symposium." *The Way* 20 (1980), pp. 87–139.

Schanz, John P. *The Sacraments of Life and Worship* (Milwaukee: Bruce, 1966).

———. *A Theology of Community* (Washington, D.C.: University of America Press, 1977).

Schillebeeckx, Edward. *Christ, the Sacrament of the Encounter with God* (New York: Sheed & Ward, 1963).

Schillebeeckx, Edward, and Boniface Willems (eds.). *The Sacraments in General: A New Perspective, Concilium*, Vol. 31 (New York: Paulist Press, 1968).

Schineller, P. "A Fresh Approach to The Sacraments," *Cross and Crown* 21 (1969), pp. 193–200.

Segundo, Juan (S.J.). *The Sacraments Today*, trans. John Drury (New York: Maryknoll, 1974).

Siedlecki, E. "Renewing The Sacraments," *Chicago Studies* 8 (September 1969), pp. 3–15.

Taylor, Michael J. (S.J.) (ed.). *The Sacraments: Readings in Contemporary Sacramental Theology* (New York: Alba House, 1981).

Tracy, David, Hans Küng, and Johann Metz (eds.). *Toward Vatican III* (New York: Seabury, 1978).

Tsirpanlis, Constantine N. "Ecumenical Consensus on the Church, the Sacraments, Ministry and Reunion," *Diakonia* 13:2 (1978), pp. 120–35.

Vagaggini, Cipriano. *The Dimensions of the Liturgy*, trans.

Leonard Doyle and W.A. Jurgens (from 4th Italian ed.; ed. revised and augmented by author) (Collegeville, Minn.: Liturgical Press, 1976).

Vaillancourt, Raymond. *Toward a Renewal of Sacramental Theology*, trans. Matthew J. O'Connell (Collegeville, Minn.: Liturgical Press, 1979).

White, James F. *Introduction to Christian Worship* (Nashville, Tenn.: Abingdon, 1980).

Wicks, Jared (S.J.) "The Sacraments: A Catechism for Today," in *An American Catholic Catechism*, ed. George Dyer (New York: Seabury Press, 1975).

Worgul, George S., Jr. *From Magic to Metaphor* (New York: Paulist Press, 1980).

INTRODUCTION AND CHAPTER ONE

Allmen, J.J. von. *Worship: Its Theology and Practice* (New York.: Oxford University Press, 1965).

Bouyer, Louis. *Rite and Man* (Notre Dame, Ind.: University of Notre Dame Press, 1963).

Bro, Bernard. "Man and the Sacraments: The Anthropological Substructure of the Christian Sacraments," in *Concilium*, Vol. 31 (New York: Paulist Press, 1968), pp. 33–50.

Collins, Mary. "Ritual Symbols and Ritual Process," *Worship* 50:4 (1976), pp. 336–46.

Douglas, Mary. *Natural Symbols* (London: Barrie and Rockliff, 1970).

Dulles, Avery (S.J.). "Symbolic Structure of Revelation," *Theological Studies* 41 (March 1980), pp. 51–73.

Erikson, Erik. "The Development of Ritualization," in *The Religious Situation* (Boston: Beacon Press, 1968), pp. 711–33.

Gallen, John. "The Necessity of Ritual," *The Way* 13 (October 1973), pp. 270–82.

George, Gordon. "The Sociology of Ritual," *The American Catholic Sociological Review* 17:1 (1956), pp. 117–30.

Jones, Paul D. *Rediscovering Ritual* (New York: Newman, 1973).

King, Winston L. *Introduction to Religion* (New York: Harper and Row, 1968).

Langer, Susanne. *Philosophy in a New Key* (New York: Mentor, 1951).

Lawler, M. "Christian Rituals: An Essay in Sacramental Symbolisms," *Horizons: Journal of the College Theology Society* 7 (Spring 1980).

Magee, John B. *Religion and Modern Man* (New York: Harper and Row, 1967).

Mitchell, Leonel L. *The Meaning of Ritual* (New York: Paulist Press, 1977).

Nagendra, S.P. "The Concept of Ritual in Modern Sociological Theory," (New Delhi: The Academic Journals of India, 1971).

O'Dea, Thomas. *The Sociology of Religion* (New York: Prentice-Hall, 1966).

Rahner, Karl. *Foundations of Christian Faith* (New York: Seabury Press, 1978).

———. "The Theology of the Symbol," in *Theological Investigations*, Vol. 4 (Baltimore: Helicon Press, 1966), pp. 221–52.

Ratzinger, Joseph. *Die sakramentale Begründung Christlicher Existenz*, (München-Freising: Kyrios-Verlag, 1966).

Ricoeur, Paul. "Parole et Symbole," *Revue des Sciences Religieuses* 49 (1975), pp. 142–61.

Shaughnessy, James (ed.). *The Roots of Ritual* (Grand Rapids: Eerdmans, 1973).

Sheets, J. "Symbol and Sacrament," *Worship* 41 (1967), pp. 194–210.

Wright, John H. *A Theology of Christian Prayer* (New York: Pueblo, 1979).

CHAPTER TWO

Dulles, Avery (S.J.). *Models of the Church* (New York: Doubleday, 1974).

Group of Les Dombes, "The Holy Spirit, the Church and the Sacraments," *One in Christ* 16:3 (1980), pp. 234–64.

Kucharek, Casimir. *The Sacramental Mysteries, A Byzantine Approach* (Glendale, N.J.: Alleluia Press, 1976).

Ledwith, Michael. "Indications of Mystery: The Sacraments in Salvation," *Furrow* 28 (1977), pp. 619–26; 29 (1978), pp. 38–42.

Musurillo, H. "Sacramental Symbolism and The *Mysterion* of The Early Church," *Worship* 39 (1965), pp. 265–74.

Osborne, Kenan B. "Jesus as Human Expression of the Divine Presence: Toward a New Incarnation of the Sacraments," in *The Sacraments: God's Love and Mercy Actualized*, ed. F. A. Eigo (Villanova, Pa.: Villanova University Press, 1979), pp. 29–58.

Rahner, Karl. *The Church and the Sacraments* (New York: Herder and Herder, 1962).

———. "The Word and the Eucharist," *Theological Investigations*, Vol. 4 (Baltimore: Helicon Press, 1965), pp. 253–86.

Schanz, John P. *A Theology of Community* (Washington, D.C.: University of America Press, 1977).

Schillebeeckx, Edward. *Christ, the Sacrament of the Encounter with God* (New York: Sheed and Ward, 1963).

Schmaus, Michael. *The Church as Sacrament* (Dogma, Vol. 5) (London: Sheed and Ward, 1975).

Semmelroth, Otto (S.J.). *Church and Sacrament*, trans. Emily Schossberger (Notre Dame, Ind.: Fides, 1965).

———. *Die Kirche als Ursakrament* (Frankfurt, 1952).

Senior, Donald (C.P.). "God's Creative Word at Work in our Midst: The Mystery/Sacrament of Divine Love from Genesis to Jesus," in *The Sacraments: God's Love and Mercy Actualized*, ed. F.A. Eigo (Villanova, Pa.: Villanova University Press, 1979), pp. 1–28.

CHAPTER THREE

Clark, Francis. "Grace Experience in the Catholic Tradition," *Theology Digest* 23:3 (1975), pp. 226–34.

Clark, Neville. *An Approach to the Theology of Sacraments* (London: SCM Press, 1958).

Delormé, J., P. Benoit, M. E. Boismard, et al. *The Eucharist in the New Testament*, trans. E. M. Stewart (Baltimore: Helicon Press, 1964).

Emminghaus, J.H. *The Eucharist: Essence, Form, Celebration* (Collegeville, Minn.: Liturgical Press, 1978).

Ernst, Cornelius (O.P.). *The Theology of Grace*, in *Theology Today Series*, Vol. 17 (Dublin & Cork: Mercier Press, 1974), pp. 62–94.

Fransen, Piet. "The Anthropological Dimensions of Grace," *Theology Digest*, 23:3 (1975), pp. 217–23.

————. *The New Life of Grace* (New York: Seabury Press, 1973).

Guzie, Tad. *Jesus and the Eucharist* (New York: Paulist Press, 1974).

Hellwig, Monica. "New Understanding of the Sacraments," *Commonweal* 105 (June 16, 1978), pp. 375–80.

Jones, Cheslyn, Geoffrey Wainwright, and Edward Yarnold. *The Study of Liturgy* (New York: Oxford University Press, 1978).

Käsemann, Ernst. *Commentary on Romans* (Grand Rapids, Mich.: Eerdmans, 1980).

Kavanagh, Aidan, et al. (eds.). *Made, Not Born* (Notre Dame, Ind.: University of Notre Dame Press, 1976).

————. *The Shape of Baptism* (New York: Pueblo, 1978).

Kilmartin, Edward J. (S.J.). *The Eucharist in the Primitive Church* (Englewood Cliffs, N.J.: Prentice-Hall, 1965).

Minear, P. "Some Glimpses of Luke's Sacramental Theology," *Worship* 44 (1970), pp. 322–31.

Moloney, Raymond. "The Early Church: An Hypothesis of Development," *Irish Theological Quarterly* 45:3 (1978), pp. 167–76.

Osborn, K.B. "Methodology and Christian Sacraments," *Worship* 48:9 (1974), pp. 536–49.

Rahner, Karl. "What is a Sacrament?" *Worship* 47:5 (1973), pp. 274–87.

Schnackenburg, Rudolf. *Baptism in the Thought of St. Paul* (New York: Herder and Herder, 1964).

Seasoltz, R. Kevin. *New Liturgy, New Laws* (Collegeville, Minn.: Liturgical Press, 1980).

Worden, Thomas (ed.). *Sacraments in Scripture, A Symposium* (Springfield, Ill.: Templegate, 1966).

Zimany, R.D. "Grace, Deification, and Sanctification: East and West," *Diakonia* 12 (1977), pp. 121–44.

CHAPTER FOUR

Barden, G. "The Speaking of Sacraments: Some Reflections on Ritual and Language," *Irish Theological Quarterly* 40:1 (1973), pp. 38–49.

Bausch, William J. "The Role of the Sacraments in the Formation of Faith," *The Living Light* 14 (Summer 1977), pp. 294–311.

Cooke, Bernard. *Ministry to Word and Sacraments* (Philadelphia: Fortress Press, 1976).

Fink, Peter E. "Three Languages of Christian Sacraments," *Worship* 52 (1978), pp. 561–75.

Fries, Heinrich (ed.). *Wort und Sakrament* (München: Kösel, 1966).

Hodgson, Peter C. *Jesus—Word and Presence* (Philadelphia: Fortress Press, 1978).

Kiesling, C. "From Ceremony to Communication," *Chicago Studies* 7 (September 1968), pp. 69–88.

Kilmartin, Edward J. (S.J.), "A Modern Approach to the Word of God and Sacraments of Christ: Perspectives and Principles," in *The Sacraments: God's Love and Mercy Actualized*, ed. Francis Eigo (Villanova, Pa.: Villanova University Press, 1979), pp. 59–109.

Langer, Susanne K. *Problems of Art* (New York: Scribner's, 1957).

Martinich, A.P. "Sacraments and Speech Acts," *Heythrop Journal* 16 (July 1975), pp. 289–303; 16 (Oct. 1975) pp. 405–17.

Power, David. *Ministers of Christ and His Church* (London: Chapman, 1969).

Searle, Mark. "The Narrative Quality of Christian Liturgy," in *Chicago Studies* 21:1 (1982), pp. 73–84.

Shea, William M. "Sacraments and Meaning," *American Ecclesiastical Review* 169:6 (1975), pp. 403–16.

Williams, R R (ed.). *Word and Sacrament* (London: SPCK, 1968).

Worgul, George S., Jr. *From Magic to Metaphor* (New York: Paulist Press, 1980), Chap. 8, "Word and Sacrament," pp. 129–41.

CHAPTER FIVE

Duffy, Regis (O.F.M.). "New Forms of Parish Ministry," in *Parish: A Place for Worship*, ed. Mark Searle (Collegeville, Minn.: Liturgical Press, 1981), pp. 97–118.

Kiesling, Christopher (O.P.). "Paradigms of Sacramentality," *Worship* 44 (August-September 1970), pp. 422–32.

King, R. "The Origin and Evolution of a Sacramental Formula: *Sacramentum Tantum, Res et Sacramentum, Res Tantum*," *Thomist* 31 (January 1967): pp. 21–82.

Macquarrie, John. *An Existentialist Theology* (New York: Harper and Row, 1965).

McGonigle, Thomas D. (O.P.). "The Significance of Albert the Great's view of Sacrament within Medieval Sacramental Theology," *Thomist* 44 (October 1980), pp. 560–83.

Miyakawa, T. "The Ecclesial Meaning of the *Res et Sacramentum*," *Thomist* 31 (October 1967), pp. 381–441.

Palmer, Paul (S.J.). "The Theology of the *Res et Sacramentum*," in *Readings in Sacramental Theology* (Englewood Cliffs, N.J.: Prentice-Hall, 1965).

Powers, Joseph M. (S.J.). *Eucharistic Theology* (New York: Herder and Herder, 1967).

Rahner, Karl. "Considerations on the Active Role of the Person in the Sacramental Event," *Theological Investigations*, Vol. 14 (New York: Seabury Press, 1976), pp. 161–84.

———. "How to Receive a Sacrament and Mean It," *Theology Digest* 19:3 (1971), pp. 227–34.

Schmemann, Alexander. *The World as Sacrament* (London: Darton, Longman & Todd, 1966).

Schrofner, Erich. "Grace and Experience in Rahner and Boff," *Theology Digest* 29:3 (1981), pp. 213–16.

Tracy, David. *Blessed Rage for Order* (New York: Seabury Press, 1975).

CHAPTER SIX

Cameli, Louis John. "The Spirituality of Celebration," *Chicago Studies* 16:1 (1977), pp. 63–74.

Casel, Odo. *The Mystery of Christian Worship*, trans. from German, ed. Burkhard Neunheuser (Westminster, Md.: The Newman Press, 1962).

Coffy, R., P. Valadier, and J. Streiff. *Une Église qui célèbre et qui prie* (Paris: Le Centurion, 1974).

Crichton, J.D. *Christian Celebration: The Prayer of the Church* (London: Geoffrey Chapman, 1976).

Duchesnau, Cl. *La Célébration dans le vie chretienne* (Paris: Le Centurion, 1975).

Empereur, James L. (S.J.)."Models for a Liturgical Theology," in *The Sacraments: Readings in Contemporary Sacramental Theology*, ed. Michael Taylor (S.J.) (New York: Alba House, 1981), pp. 53–70.

Fransen, P. "Sacraments as Celebrations," *Irish Theological Quarterly* 43:3 (1976), pp. 151–70.

Gallen, John. "Liturgical Celebration American Style," in *Chicago Studies* 16:1 (1977), pp. 29–44.

Guzie, Tad. *The Book of Sacramental Basics* (New York: Paulist Press, 1981), esp. Chap. 5, "The Sacramental Process," pp. 71–91.

Häring, Bernard (C.Ss.R.). *The Sacraments and Your Daily Life* (Liguori, Mo.: Liguori Publications, 1976).

Padovano, Anthony T. *Presence and Structure: A Reflection on Celebration, Worship and Faith.* (New York: Paulist Press, 1976).

Rafky, David M. "Phenomenology and Socialization: Comments on the Assumptions Underlying Socialization Theology," *Sociological Analysis* 32 (1972), pp. 7–19.

Schall, Richard V. "On Worship," *Worship* 52:6 (1978), pp. 67–76.

Scharlemann, R.P. "Theological Models and Their Construction," *The Journal of Theology* 53 (1973), pp. 65–82.

Thurian, Max. *The Eucharistic Memorial* (Richmond: John Knox Press, Vol. 1, 1980; Vol. 2, 1961).

Vaillancourt, R. "Celebration," in *Toward a Renewal of Sacramental Theology*, trans. Matthew J. O'Connell (Collegeville, Minn.: Liturgical Press, 1979), pp. 102–12.

Worgul, George S. "Celebration: A New Sacramental Model," in *From Magic to Metaphor* (New York: Paulist Press, 1980), pp. 213–21.

———. "Celebrations: Models for Sacraments," *Chicago Studies* 16 (Fall 1977), pp. 309–15.

Index

188